Parents as People:

The Family as a Creative Process

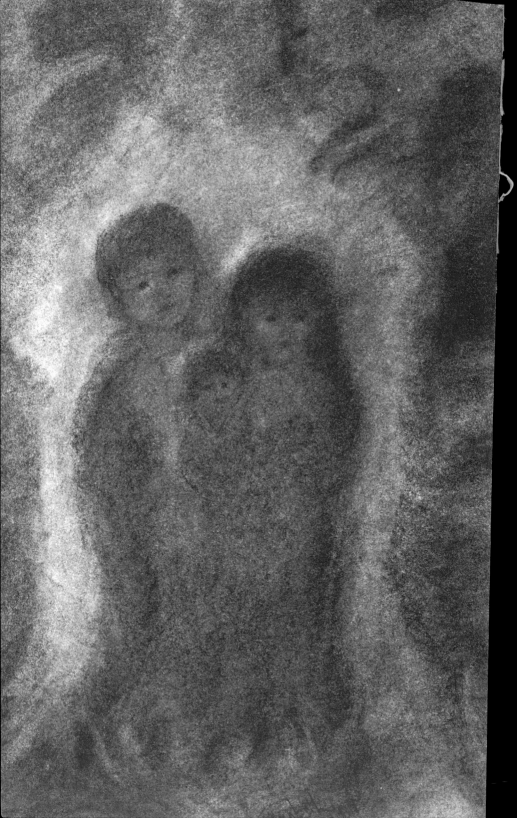

Parents as People:

The Family as a Creative Process

by: Franklin Kane

artwork: Elizabeth Keefe

Aurora Publishers

Edmonton

Acknowledgements

Every book has an author and then the many people who have helped, inspired, suffered with and lived through the experience.

My thanks and appreciation to Maureen Nelson for typing and retyping the manuscript as well as taking over the production. Also thanks to Johanne Rauscher for early editing and encouragement.

And to Evangeline for your support and for your encouragement - I thank you with love.

Text Copyright 1987 © Franklin Kane
Artwork Copyright 1987 © Elizabeth Keefe

Printed in Canada by Friesen Printers

ISBN No. 0-88925-820-1

Aurora Publishers

AURORA PUBLISHERS
7829 111 AVE
EDMONTON ALTA T5H 1L1

Table of Contents

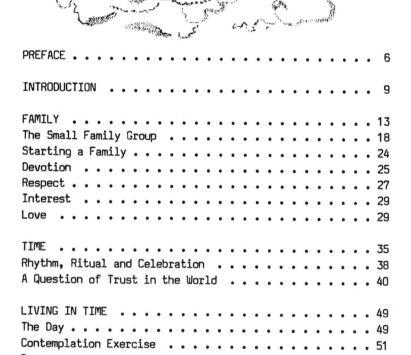

Dedication

For

Andrea
Randy
George
Sonya
Nicholette

Children who have given so much to me!

Preface

During the past twenty years I have had the privilege of giving lectures, workshops and seminars in many communities in North America. Most of these presentations have had some connection with the many Waldorf (Rudolf Steiner) schools that have come into being all over the free world.

Most of my adult life has been devoted to teaching children in Waldorf Schools from Grade One to Grade Twelve as well as to the training of prospective Waldorf teachers. In the course of this work, I have had extensive contact with parents. Over the years I have experienced a difference in the type and intensity of the questions that parents ask. In the past, there were many questions about Waldorf Education; its curriculum and methods of instruction; stages of childhood as Rudolf Steiner has indicated and how these developmental stages are to be understood; the value of this or that subject which may be taught in a Waldorf school; how these schools are organized and the role of parents in the foundation and life of a school.

More recently, there have been many more questions about the parent/child relationship: what can be done to bring the home life into harmony with the high ideals of Waldorf Education? How does the family become strengthened in order to be a more nurturing place for the child and the parents? And how do we protect children from the many unhealthy and damaging influences of modern culture such as the media, electronic encroachments into the home, unwholesome commercial products that are pushed at us through clever advertising? How to stand against the many dubious standards and values that are propagated in general society against which many people feel impotent?

On the positive side, these questions show an increasing awareness of the problems that we face today. A growing number of people are willing to devote themselves to the struggle for more consciousness in many areas and aspects of their lives.

Over the years, I have found that people are asking more questions about what they can do to make a better environment for themselves and their children. They are still vitally interested in knowing about the ideals and practices of Waldorf Education while recognizing that the very foundation in relation to their families is the home that they create.

The content of this short book comes from several basic sources. It arises out of my experiences as a parent whose oldest children are themselves professional people. Twenty-six years of teaching and the close relationships formed with many children and their families has been an invaluable source of information about the challenges, pitfalls and successes in the art of parenting. Rudolf Steiner's vast scope of work has been a continual inspiration and my guide both as an educator and in the far more difficult task of knowing myself. Rudolf Steiner's Anthroposophy (Spiritual Science) out of which the Waldorf schools have grown is a vast body of knowledge in which Steiner has helped people to see the world of matter and the world of psyche (soul) in the context of the spiritual world whose forces are everywhere present.[1]Even more important is the moral, Christian path of self and spiritual development which Rudolf Steiner has presented. Through all of his work, one may find the deepest respect for the freedom and dignity of the individual. Never is there any coercion or persuasion. Instead, one will find a gentle and steady encouragement for people to work on their own individual path. Steiner's work is difficult and perhaps that is the way it should be. Without the extra effort, are the results ever as sweet?

Introduction

In marriage and in the forming of a family we have the opportunity to express our most profound creativity. In the following pages a number of major themes to which we as parents need to give attention will be addressed. This is not, by any means, intended to be a complete 'How to be a Good Parent' or 'Steps and Methods in Creating a Family,' recipe book. While there are many practical suggestions throughout the book, the main aim has been to provoke one's thoughts and feelings and to inspire the reader to discover new ways of looking at what lives within and without. I hope this book may be a catalyst for the reader's own creativity in relation to being a parent and in the formation of a family which is the womb out of which the raising of children may happen.

No amount of rules, methods and techniques can create anything of value without there living in the creator a sense for the aesthetic. This may come about when there lives in the soul, ideas, imaginations and even inspirations which fertilize and hopefully fructify a creative impulse.

To be an artist is no easy task. In fact it is ninety-nine percent perspiration and one percent inspiration (and imagination.) An artist's life is one of devotion to bringing into the outer world an expression of what lives in the inner world. The Artist's task is not to replicate nature; for the original cannot be improved. Instead the challenge for the artist is to transform the inner image; the archetype represented by the single moment in nature, into something that is more than itself.

If we think of the process of being a parent as an artistic challenge, the medium that is our work is the human being. What can be more awe inspiring? Our creation is a continuation of what the gods have wrought. We bring to fruition the seeds that have been planted; the idea (in a Platonic sense) becomes manifest in flesh and blood. Surely this is a mighty task; greater than Leonardo da Vinci's Last Supper, Michaelangelo's Sistine Chapel or all of Shakespeare's great plays. And we start off with little training and not much recognition for the artistic talent we might have. In the end we will not have a museum piece but a growing, changing and evolving human being who may hardly give us credit, for our handiwork. Yet an artist is the creative image that we need as parents.

Today, more than ever, we need to develop an artistic attitude and feeling in order to balance the overly intellectual and utilitarian approach to life. The scientific revolution of the past several centuries has led to phenomenal achievements in industry, business and society. The general feeling that yet another invention would solve the problems we face has usually lead to new inventions and new problems - a seemingly endless chain of events. In this whole process, the human being has gradually been moved from the center of creation to the sidelines as a mere accident of evolution. This is an interesting paradox for as we have been moved to the side, humanity, as a whole, has also become more greedy and rapacious in dealing with the world of nature. Our general irresponsibility has lead to massive ecological crises and to crippling societal and personal problems.

Many old forms, institutions and traditions have decayed and rightly so, because they haven't been able to meet the new situations which confront us. The difficulty has been creating new and relevant institutions which meet the needs of the present. As we have become more cut off from nature and more alienated from religion, tradition and our spiritual origins, we have found it painful to meet some of our basic needs in a gentle, healing and humane way.

Our task is to create new social forms and institutions which will meet the needs of our present age. In order to do this, we need to bring our creativity to bear on the new social conditions. This is needed in every realm - the work place, education, government and the home. The larger social institutions demand concerted efforts and massive changes of consciousness by many people working together. The results cannot be expected in a short period of time.

It is in the social institution of the family that we

11

have the possibility of bringing changes that are health giving in the more immediate present. Here, we can begin to change our lives and regain some degree of sanity in a world that has so many pathological aspects. What we do within the family; the home we create, is perhaps more important than any massive reforms. It is in the home that the first nurturing of the young child takes place and if the parents are healthy and the mood of the home is alive and creative,then <u>one</u> of the building blocks of society is solid and strong. It is from this kind of healthy center that rays of light and sanity may stream forth to the rest of society.

Family

What do you think when the word 'family' is mentioned? Mother, father, child? Grandparents, parents, children?? Aunts, Uncles, Grandparents, parents, children? Foster parents, children?

All of the above? Some of them? Or, none of these?

So often our view of family is colored by our own experiences, our own upbringing, or perhaps what society is telling us about family, in the latest magazines, television talk shows, and popular books that seem to be ever recurring.

At the outset, several things of a general nature need to be said about the family. Family is the archetypal social form - whether in the animal world or in the human world. It is that form of coming together into groups which, in large part, is focused on the raising of children (the next generation), caring for the old (the last generation), and preserving, protecting and feeding of the present generation. The family is basic unit of socialization where individuals are called upon to give and to receive, to express themselves to others, to learn from others, to cooperate, and to divide tasks and responsibilities. Here is the place where children learn the language, rules, mores, styles, customs and ways of the society into which they are born.

13

We can see the family as a second 'womb' for the children. Within the mother's womb they are protected and nurtured. With birth and the emergence into the larger world, the individual members within the family structure hold, protect, nourish, nurture and educate the children. That is the general structure, but it is the individuals within the family who may make all the difference. Just as a healthy body (womb) makes a great deal of difference to the developing embryo, so too, does the health of the family structure and the individuals within it make all the difference to the soul of the growing child.

There is no one 'model' family. Different cultures and different ages have produced a wide variety of family models, most of which have proved successful in proportion to the health and stability of the individual and society within which it has functioned. Even within our own culture, there is a wonderful diversity of family types, and if we were to consider even the last generation or two, we would be multiplying the variety endlessly. Although I have had most of my experience with the so-called nuclear family, I have also had experience of enough different styles to realize that the actual family structure takes second place to the individuals who join and make up the family. In other words, almost any structure or grouping can work to make up a family, but its success is most dependent on the state of health, the good will, the sense of cooperation and respect, and the sense of purpose with which they can relate. This does not mean that everything in a family will be "peaches and cream" or that there may not be conflict or struggle. In fact the healthiest model we can present our children is adults who are honestly struggling to find themselves individually and in conjunction with their partners are finding purpose in their lives.

While many examples will come from a father, mother, children (nuclear) family, no judgments are made about other types of family units. Almost everything said will be applicable to all styles and types of families.

The 'ideal' family includes a man and a woman as the best representatives of the masculine and feminine principles. The successful marriage or union where a man and woman share responsibility, love one another, cooperate and relate to each other in a healthy, open way gives the children of that family the best possible images for their own growth and development. Whether the father and mother are part of a tightly built nuclear family or within the context of a larger extended family is not nearly as important as the fact that there are strong, healthy male and female models. The single parent family, so prevalent today, while offering warmth, love and caring, often lacks the balance of male/female influences, and the full spectrum of adult interaction that the child can emulate later in life. It may be said that single parents do develop, out of themselves, a more conscious balance of masculine and feminine forces which may compensate for being alone. We should also be aware of the new family structures that have arisen in the last decade or so that come out of second and third marriages where there are 'his' children, 'her' children, 'their' children, ex-wives, ex-husbands, step-children, half-sisters, half-brothers, and so on. In a certain way, this is a form of extended family and there are many cases where it works beautifully. There are also many underlying tensions because of the formerly unsuccessful marriages and a need to relate across the different lifestyles and different viewpoints which initially broke down the original marriages.

At the present time, we particularly have freedom to choose the size and form of the family unit. In the past, culture and conditions dictated that one did what one's parents did before. Now, there are many people who are consciously searching for what they feel is most suitable for their own lifestyle. Not so very long ago, the rural setting of many, and the larger houses that were available, set the basis for the form of the so-called extended family. Here, several generations lived under one roof; grandparents, parents, children, and perhaps an uncle, aunt or cousin or two might have made up the family group. It often took many hands to do all the chores necessary in the pre-electric gadget days. The littlest one may have been cared for by siblings, an aunt or a grandparent, as mother was busy supervising the household.

How different a picture that is from the mobile, transient, nuclear family of the last several generations who on the average (at least in California) move once every two years. This family unit usually has parents and children and because of the frequent moves, often has few deep roots outside the small family. Friends are transient, as are houses, furniture, schools. Suburbia demands conventional furniture to fit conventional spaces. Any amount of extra room or time to accumulate and create individual style is limited.

Schools, shops, clubs, and backyards are generally
uniform so that the transient family can fit in wherever
it happens to land for its relatively short stay. This
style of life (or lack of it) has taken its great toll
on a generation or two of us in a number of ways: It
often cuts us off from our larger family ties;
grandparents, uncles, aunts, cousins, sisters
and brothers are spread all across the
country and what had once been a
gathering of the 'clan' can
rarely happen anymore.

Putting down roots has become very
difficult. Friends for adults or children
are barely made when it is once again time to go.
The social interaction of deep long lasting and intimate
relationships are exchanged for the more superficial,
quick and passing friendship. Hard work and effort are
needed to develop a deep relationship and often the
question arises: 'Is it really worth it?'

The Small Family Group

The small family group has been thrown
on itself and this has created many
pressures and demands for which mother
and/or father are inadequately prepared.
The sheer logistics of earning a living, running
the household, fulfilling social obligations and duties
in a far-flung setting where one is always dependent
upon a car has created tremendous challenges. Life for
many has become a consistent whirl of activity –
perpetual motion – and there seems no way to get off the
constantly moving wheel; nor is there any inward
nourishment to be derived from staying on it. Many of us
have begun to rebel from this seemingly empty, plastic
life and have tried to slow the whirl and add meaning to
the life we lead.

The challenge to slow down and add quality to quantity
is difficult, especially when society continually
reinforces the image of being beautiful, quick,
charming, efficient, caring and sexy. Women and men are
both in this fast lane and little is said about the
family relationship and the slow nurturing that goes
into being a good parent. Parenting and being in intense
relationship to another human being are not "fast lane"
activities. Relationship, unlike roast beef, cannot be
microwaved; a slow burning even and steady warmth are
needed to bring a well cooked tenderness which
penetrates through and through. This slow and thorough
simmering can best happen within the container of the
family.

Our children first experience their own sense of self in family and the mood that is created within it. Whether it be the new form of an extended family that includes friends, relatives, and assorted and sundry drop-ins, the commune, or the tighter more conscious small, nuclear family, our challenge is to bring meaning, sanity and health to the life we lead. Therefore, the quality of family life and those things we express and do within the confines of our home do much to mold ourselves and our children. If our home is indeed our 'castle' then we must take on the responsibility of the old king, who with all seriousness and earnestness applied himself to making his kingdom a good, happy place in which to live. We have lived complacently with this myth of the castle for generations. But now we must be careful because the family is not fully self-sufficient, nor, in fact, has it ever been to the extent to which we have been made to believe.[2]

Today more than ever, the family is dependent on outside forces which to a certain extent are even beyond the parent's control. At a time when the family has few deep roots and is generally weak and over-extended; when it has fewer church and neighborhood ties, it has, ironically become all the more dependent on the outside than ever before. The difference now is that the 'outside' comes right into the midst of the family in the guise of media (television, videos, magazines, radio, records, advertising.) Governmental pressures, schools, peer group pressure and economic and social forces also strongly act out on the family.

With so many more mothers working outside of the home, families are now facing the increased challenges of these hard-to-control social influences. The traditional role of standard bearer is no longer easily kept by mother and father. No wonder there is frustration on the part of parents who try to maintain a high ideal, and yet see their children exposed to the shifting, slick and commercial values packaged in clever ways. Generally, today, the family plays a diminished role in health care, education, counselling and the setting of moral standards. An extended discussion of this would take us too far afield, but a short consideration is at least necessary.

Even a century ago relatively few people went to school for more than a few years and then only long enough to learn to read and write. Schools have steadily taken on broader functions so that in this generation they (particularly the public schools) are the dumping ground for all sorts of 'orientation' to modern culture that once was the responsibility of the home. Driver education, sex education, cooking classes, babycare classes, consumer advice classes, chequebook balancing (as part of basic math); along with art appreciation, literature, psychology, sociology, are offered at most high schools. Although the student achievement levels continually slide downward in basic learning skills, there is this growing proliferation of courses that is either replacing what is not in the home or challenging what the parents may be presenting in the home.

In health care, during the last century, we witnessed the situation changing from perhaps seeing a doctor once or twice in one's life, to becoming quite dependent on doctors and healers of one sort or another. Whereas mother or grandmother used to be able to diagnose most ordinary ailments and deal with them on the spot, most parents now seem to have lost the instinct or self-confidence to deal with even a simple cold or a fever without calling the doctor for the advice that we already know will be given. Because of our rushed, frenetic lives and the growing feeling that we have no time to be sick, we have forgotten many sound, home remedies which allowed common illnesses to run their course. We often feel at the mercy of the sophisticated medical practitioner who uses sophisticated medicines. We tend to feel helpless without the advice of the 'experts.' So here again, the role of the parent is changed and reduced to the person who can make the doctor's appointment and get the family there on time.

This question of health care has even expanded to where governments have challenged (and usually won) court battles for custody of children whose parents, because of religious persuasion have refused certain medical procedures such as blood transfusions. Social Welfare departments vie with parents for children's custody. In many circumstances parents now have to prove their competence and fight for the right to raise their own children. Some heart rending and complicated situations requiring the wisdom of Solomon now face modern society.

We could go on with many more examples of how the parent's role in the family has changed and evolved, and how, in fact, the family itself has taken on a new relationship to the world around it. By now, it should be clear that the pictures and ideas that have been passed down regarding what the family is, need seriously to be re-examined. Drastic changes in social conditions have resulted in the weakening of the sense of confidence in the 'old' style family. Parents are blamed for being selfish, immature, unwilling or unable to cope with the new conditions. There have even been persuasive arguments to do away with the nuclear family saying it is inefficient and ineffectual; replacing the care of children at home with institutional day-care centers which could take children from three months on from eight a.m., to six p.m., six days a week.[3]

There is a crisis of confidence in people as parents, potential parents and members of families because of their own poor experiences and the loudly proclaimed criticism of the 'old ways' of doing things. Our current craze of nostalgia is only now beginning to look at some of the old standards, morals and ways as valuable in the same way that old furniture, books, nick-nacks and clothes have value. While the old does have value, it can no longer be a question of going back because society, culture and technology have gone forward.

We are caught between old and new, past and present, known and unknown. We often want to give up the old ways, but have nothing with which to replace them. We want to be new, trendy and in step with modern approaches. We cann't go back to the past, the present is too elusive, so what about going forward, into the future?

But forward toward what?

Our challenge is to find what is of value, both in the old and in the new because it has a universal value. Whether something is made to appear old or new is unimportant. What is important and relevant is its sense of lasting value.

As individuals, we need to develop confidence in ourselves and a good, sound judgment based on healthy instinct, sharp thinking and serious reflection. More important, we have to develop our heart forces. The warmth of heart needs be added to the light of thinking in order to come to a true moral imagination (picture) of what is required of us. We have to have far more consciousness about ourselves and our relationship to the world around us. In other words we need to be developing our relationship to soul and spirit; to our inner world and the unseen world as well as to the outer world we see and experience with our senses.

When we develop insight - the ability to look within - we then have the possibility to come into psychological relationship with traditional and lasting values. At a time when we have little trust in our own instincts and feelings for what is right and wrong or good and bad for ourselves and for the world, it is essential that we get to know our own soul with its complexity. If we don't know ourselves, how can we really know the world? If we are directed by the outer world and its changing standards we end up bobbing and tossing on the sea - directionless and sea sick.

Starting A Family

Embarking on parenthood - starting a family - is one of
the oldest of human activities dating back to Adam and
Eve, and yet at this point in human history we have lost
our way. The fog has closed in and we are wary of taking
even the first step towards that commitment to marriage,
to long-term relationships, to the responsibilities that
face us.

Yes, there has been hypocrisy in marriage; many family
structures have been far from ideal. Recent generations
have broken new ground dramatically by asking many of
the basic and needed questions. There are few
assumptions left and we are looking at each and every
part of our lives through a hopefully clear glass. Let
us hope that we don't miss what has been and is positive
in human experience; that in this present day search for
new and better ways
to be true to ourselves,
and to meet more adequately
the quickly changing world
in which we live, we don't
forget to look for the lasting
values that have guided
people through the ages.

It would be presumptuous to try and list those values in
general, but in focusing on the family, I would attempt
to list several qualities that do seem vitally important
regardless of time, place, or style of family. What are
these qualities of family life that are so important?

Devotion

Devotion: to devote, devout, devoted. There is a religious connotation to this word and that is as it should be. We could describe devotion as a commitment to our 'higher' cause or origin. True devotion comes out of a consciously free decision to commit oneself to the service of a 'higher' cause. (Higher is used in the sense of something that is noble or worth striving towards.)

Can we put the family on such a pedestal? Most definitely yes, but remember that doesn't mean a fixed idea of the family structure and form. That is up to you. Whatever family form you choose is one that needs to be infused with the ideal of devotion to family life, not in the abstract but in the genuine human way. If the family is a basic social unit, then it has the possibility to be the proving ground for human interaction. Even two adults living together create a family. (I knew of a bachelor who lived with his pet bobcat named Mr. Livingston which he considered his family. He served this family of his with more love, respect and devotion than many other people seem to treat their 'conventional' family situations.) The devotion is not to an abstraction; it is to the highest ideal of humanity - the respect, love, dignity, reciprocity and caring of one person for another. To be devoted to or at least attempting to serve this ideal already puts us on the road to openness in family life.

We have all seen the 'Jewish Mother' type who is so completely devoted to the family that all within it may feel overly mothered and smothered. That is a form of devotion filled with "mother love" that literally knows no bounds. While it lacks discernment, sublety and room for freedom and movement on the part of others in the family, it is probably preferable to the sterility and emptiness of a family that shows little or no devotion.

Devotion to the family in the true sense will mean that there is a strong willingness to see the process of family life through its good times and bad; its successes and failures; its crises and resolutions. This means the commitment to that grouping of people so that each may find a sense for humanity and selfhood. True devotion suggests having the commitment to care for and help and support as best we can, each person, no matter what the differences.

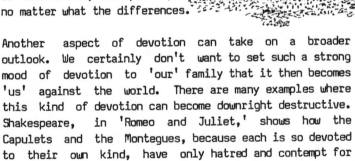

Another aspect of devotion can take on a broader outlook. We certainly don't want to set such a strong mood of devotion to 'our' family that it then becomes 'us' against the world. There are many examples where this kind of devotion can become downright destructive. Shakespeare, in 'Romeo and Juliet,' shows how the Capulets and the Montegues, because each is so devoted to their own kind, have only hatred and contempt for others.

The broader aspect of devotion needs to take in a view of the world in which each of us has a devotion to making this world of ours a better place to live. Does this sound too idealistic? Not at all. We certainly "don't live by bread alone." We need ideals and we need ethical and moral principles to guide our lives. As we develop these more strongly, for ourselves, we find that the family of which we are a part can become more enriched, more interesting, more alive with a sense of purpose. Devotion to the family, its process, its striving; that does have meaning. A further devotion to important causes and issues in the outside world allows something to flow back into the family structure which may enrich us.

Respect

Respect can take many forms. We often tend to view respect as from a mountain top. We look down and see the differences between people and their styles and ways and can say: "Yes, there is room for all kinds in the world." What is meant here is the true respect for others that comes from involvement and commitment rather than from distance.

Within any family, there needs to be respect for the individuality of each person, recognizing that each has his own individual destiny as well as the connection with this group. Only when we can come to the point of inwardly experiencing our individuality are we able to realize that everyone has that spark of the eternal within themselves. We can then have true involvement, devotion and respect for the other members of our family; for then we are not trying to change our wife, husband, child or parent into our own image. For fathers particularly, this can be a problem and a challenge as they often see their children as reflections of themselves and can love them for what they do in the

27

world; whereas mothers may love their children in a far less conditional way. Too many mothers and fathers see their children as beings to be molded into their image and they may be hurt and disappointed when the child expresses his individuality by choosing a 'different' career or that the child's personality, temperament, interests, or other tastes may be quite different and unexpected.

Our devotion and our love needs to be more freely given; we need to love and to respect the inner being rather than what we want the outer manifestation of personality to be. We need to work at helping instill a sense of respect for the various strengths and weaknesses of each family member. Often, there can be such sharp and intense rivalry between siblings or children and parents or parent and parent. To respect and support those strengths or weaknesses may often open the field so that we can admit our weaknesses and give and get the help and support that can be forthcoming from the other family members. While competition may be appropriate at certain points in our society, it is cooperation and respect by which we really thrive and flourish. Competition encourages winners and losers. In a family, caring and respect along with cooperation encourages each person to do their best. The family is most alive and successful when each family member is "winning" in some way. Competition narrows the field while cooperation and respect broaden the field and allow for diversity, exploration and creativity.

Interest

To have interest means to 'enter in.' Entering in may take time, effort, and even sacrifice on our part. Can I put aside my own endeavors, interests and preoccupations in order to enter into what my mate, child, sibling is doing and being? Interest (just as a saving bank pays) 'can grow and be compounded daily.' We may draw interest from those around us. If we can put aside our 'self' for the moment to enter into the other, we open ourselves to the possibility of learning and gaining from the other.

It is not a matter of condescending or being interested out of 'duty' but rather of being interested out of sincere interest. We want to know what the other is thinking, feeling and doing. In that way it makes the sharing of life's struggles more meaningful. We don't live with strangers, and in order to know one another, we must take an interest in each family member. Interest becomes the building stone of the family structure and helps to form the connection of one to another. It takes much time and effort to ferret out (from each) what is really going on, not out of idle curiosity, but out of a deep inner yearning so that we might continue to build a respect and love for the other which then allows the devotion to the family to develop and mature.

Love

Love is an obvious part of family life which is what usually has brought the family into being. It may begin with infatuation, physical attraction, love-at-first-sight, or in any number of ways, but by the time it has come to the making of a long-term commitment, to being together and raising a family, a process has taken place. Again it would take us too far afield to go into a long treatise on love, and its many levels and stages, but it is, after all, the cornerstone of the initial relationship.

Romantic love may be the catalyst: that which inflames the heart and has gradually infused the thinking and will of the couple. With the 'settling down' into the family with its trials and tribulations, challenges and problems, we may sometimes wonder where all the love has gone, or even if it was really ever there. We have to think back (sometimes with great effort) to those 'other times' when life and love were so beautiful and magical. Our challenge is to allow that love to evolve, to take its different and varied forms. That first blush of romantic love can be so selfish, indulgent and misleading. Often, at that time, we are more in love with the idea of love and the images and fantasies that we create. We can be in love with love. That isn't a bad thing but it usually isn't enough to carry us far into the future.

Faced with the crying baby, groceries, bills, laundry and the broken toaster, we can easily forget those early images of romantic love. Now, we have constantly and consciously to renew, not the old love, but the steadily growing new love based on growing intimacy, shared experience, respect, admiration and interest in the other. We also need to create the time and conditions to enhance the romantic feeling that started it all. Our love now needs to be shared as the family grows: the more love we give and share, the more we have flowing from us and toward us.

The love for children should not be in conflict with the love that one has and shares with one's mate. It is the original reason for it, and the children are an extension of that love. Yes, there is limited time and energy while there are growing demands of all types upon us, but that is not a competition to the deep inner feelings and connections between man and wife. We need to distinguish between those outer demands and the inner connection and realize that as individuals we need to be constantly growing.

Love for our children certainly cannot be romantic, sentimental, or possessive. Love has to be focused on the inner being of the child. We need to be strong and mature enough to transcend their dirty diapers, being awakened at three a.m., the 'no' stage, and even adolescence.

To have the image that your children chose you, chose to incarnate into the physical body that you and your mate had to offer, and chose to share in your life's path with all that it might bring, can certainly help to get you away from that destructive aspect of possessive love that some parents have for their children. We don't own our children, nor have we created them fully. We have allowed them to enter the world and we have supplied the primary physical home (the bare body) along with some of the strengths and weaknesses of our own hereditary stream. We also supply them with a home, family and environment in which to grow and develop. Aside from heredity and environment, each of our children comes with their own distinct personality for which we can take neither blame nor credit. Our challenge is to love our children for what they are and will become and not for what we want them to be. This can make our love all the more whole and complete as it then isn't as fraught with expectations whether real or fantastic. We need to realize the importance of our role as parents and the importance of our love in a caring, nurturing, protecting and loving environment out of which the child may grow.

True love asks nothing in return. We don't love another because of what it may do for us, or for what we may get in return. Our love for another in the highest form needs to be freely given. Needless to say our love for our children is quite different from romantic love and the emotional response that it gives us in return. The infant literally grows healthy and thrives on our love for it. Love and its natural expressions of touching can make all the difference (even of life and death) for the infant. Later on we also need to continue that same intensity of love even in the face of rebellion, arguments, disagreements and disappointments. It is our love, truly deep seated and freed from the child's momentary response to us, that can be of value for both the child and for us as parents and people. It is the rock upon which the whole edifice of the family is built. In fact it is one of the highest values of humanity. It is the impulse that Buddha and Christ have brought to us. Our challenge is to truly internalize this love so that it may flow.

Yet we can't allow ourselves to be blinded by the love or to be so sentimentally in love with our own children that we are unable to see anything wrong with them. Our true love will enable us to see problems and take strong stands where necessary in the upbringing of our children. It will make us protective and yet not blindly

32

so. It will not prevent us from doing what in our good judgment as adults and parents we feel needs to be done, even when it may momentarily displease our child.

Love does not mean never saying 'no' to our child, or never having conflict or disagreement, or never deserting our own judgment or authority where it is appropriate. Love can mean setting great challenges for our children or our mate; for setting standards, for expecting from them the very best that they can do. It means at times that out of our caring and our love we don't take the easiest course, but rather that we resolve to struggle together for what we all know down deep to be the highest and the best. In many talks with teenagers I have heard comments such as these:

"I know that my parents love me, but if only they had set limits for me or had been consistent..."

"I often feel that the only way my parents seem to express their love for me is to buy and give me things. What I had wanted was to experience them."

"My parents seem afraid to stand up to me as if they thought that I might love them less. Now all I have is resentment for my being spoiled."

Love can show itself in so many ways. We can touch, express ourselves verbally, give presents, be attentive, and do deeds of love. There is no one way or fixed formula, but it does need to be expressed in ways which are appropriate to the situation. We cannot buy love, nor cajole it, nor bribe it; we cannot convince someone to love us. We need to express love freely, for and to the other, out of our deepest impulse. We need to act

33

for the higher love bond. That, sometimes, takes courage, as it is risky to step out and expose ourselves and do what we feel needs doing out of our love for the other. This also needs to be balanced by the respect for the freedom of the other person as well. For our children and our family, we need to reckon with love as the mortar that holds the other building blocks of family together. We need to explore this in an open and frank way even when we feel exposed and threatened by that exposure. As with so much else in our life, love - both giving and receiving - needs to be tended and nurtured. It needs caring and watering and weeding. We must be the ever careful guardians and gardeners for this within the family.

The remainder of this book will focus upon the various aspects of how these qualities - devotion, respect, interest and love - are the basis of our family relationship. When they are truly a part of us and our approach to life, then we can have the strength, courage and convictions to see through the challenges we encounter in life.

Time

Backward, turn backward, oh time in your flight,
Make me a child just for tonight.[4]

In this and the following section dealing with 'Space,'
the question of the world in which we live is being
addressed. That doesn't mean only the present social
situation but rather the actual physical world that all
material life inhabits.

As physical beings, we live within these two dimensions
of time and space which give us our measuring rods
towards life.[5]

Of course, there are many variables in these two
dimensions, but generally speaking, they are reliable
contexts in which to live. We can count on yesterday,
today and tomorrow as we can on near and far, up and
down, big and small. For the child, time and space has
quite other meanings in context than they do for the
adult. Differences occur because of physical size, sense
focus, experience, and so on. For instance, most

three-year-olds still refer to anything happening in the past as 'yesterday' regardless of the fact that it was a day, a week or a month ago. We all know how difficult it is to explain to our youngsters that they will have to 'wait a little while until we get there.' A little while may be a virtual eternity for a child who basically lives in the 'here and now' and has little relationship to past and future in the same context as the grown-up.

What is essential to remember is that as children grow into their physical bodies and into gradual consciousness, they also gradually come into contact with time and space in innumerable ways. How we, as parents, order the surroundings and the time into which our children's life flows will greatly affect their sense of well-being and general connection with the world.

Time is, fortunately, not just an onrushing stream through which we push; it does have its ups and downs, its ebbs and flows. In order to appreciate the variations of time, we once again need to distinguish the obvious difference between quantity and quality. Mechanical time does go on and on. The metronome that every music student has used can tortuously attest to this. The beat goes on and on and on, steadily, relentlessly; however, the music needs to undulate and breathe, to become alive. While practising, one may need a mechanical beat, but to make the music a 'work of art' one may have to vary the time and infuse it with the quality of life. The technician and the artist; quantity and quality; physical and biological laws; mechanical time and human rhythm, form a basic and healthy polarity in life which ultimately, in all of us, forms a comprehensive whole.

We can experience time in minute amounts or in large doses. There is geologic time measured in millions of years, or insect time measured in minutes and hours. Many flies live four hours - from birth to death! A race may be won by a tenth of a
second, or we may
speculate that it
was ten or fifteen
million years ago
that some
geological
event took place.

Associated with time
is also the question
of rhythm. Time
itself; the
mechanical, ongoing,
relentless time, can
march, run, gallop,
crawl, fly or even stand
still but it is all in the
'eyes of the beholder.'

Time keeps going, but its
rate, pulse, rhythm and quality
is up to us to experience and judge. All living
beings exist within a rhythm. The plants are subject to
the course of the year and the course of the day/night
rhythm. Animals live strongly within the seasons and the
daily rhythms. Human beings have the possibility to be
less dependent on the natural rhythms, and in recent
times have steadily turned their backs on nature's time
in favor of 'man-made' time. We can ice skate in summer,
swim in winter, eat fresh strawberries in January and

dance through the night. Animals, on the other hand come awake during the day and sleep at night, or sleep during the day and come awake at night. Whatever their pattern, it is generally unbroken, regular and predictable.

While we, as modern adults, may take advantage of the freedom of choice available to us in the activities we choose, the food we eat and the time we sleep, we can never completely turn our backs on natural rhythms: women menstruate on a lunar cycle (approximately 28 days); many people die between midnight and four a.m. which is the ebb tide of the day; our bodily temperatures are highest in the evening and lowest in the morning. We do live within the rhythms of the heavens and the earth, and are subject to their effect even though we may consciously try to ignore them.

Rhythm, Ritual and Celebration

Time moves in several ways. While 'marching on' steadily, it does so in a rhythmic way. There are twenty-four hours in a day, seven days in a week. There are cycles of time, in rhythmic patterns, upon which we count. In fact, it is the natural rhythms which give us a sense of security in a changing, unpredictable world. To know that the sun will rise, that the moon will once again be full, that winter will merge into the gentle blossoming spring, gives us a sense of stability within movement. On a personal level, we each have our own rhythms; the pulse rate and respiration that are basic and yet individual. How we sleep and how much we sleep, how often we are hungry, our attention span, and so on, all have a relation to time and have a rhythmic aspect within us. It is well known amongst long distance runners that establishing a

38

steady, comfortable pace will carry one further than running in fits and starts. A laborer can do hours of hard work once he has caught the rhythm of the work. Have you ever listened to the rhythm of a carpenter hammering nails or sawing wood?

Rhythm is the carrying element that can heal and maintain and give endurance even to the hardest of tasks. In olden days, there were strongly rhythmic chants, songs, poems which would be recited in unison as men toiled on ships, in mines or in the fields, or as women churned butter, baked bread, or spun and wove cloth. We have some remnants of these chants even today in sea chanties and work songs which are now seldom sung except for recreation but which once had a serious purpose to unify the work rhythms of the people who toiled.

It is rhythm that is the first element of making more of time than the bull blindly rushing into the China shop of the future. While rhythm can also become quite mechanical, it at least is the basis upon which we can enter the time frame in an organic, living sense.

All life processes have their rhythm; the challenge is to find the secret of rhythm most suitable to us.

Children are much more sensitive to the whole ebb and flow of time and as parents, we need to become ever more conscious of rhythmic time and the effects it has on our children. For the child to live in a rhythmic pattern already gives, in an unconscious way, the sense of anticipation and security that is so important to health giving vitality. For example just think that if we, as adults, had no idea when our next meal were to be served or when we were expected at work, or when we could take the bus or train home from work, how chaotic our inner disposition would be. As adults, we rely on some rhythmic aspects to carry us forward in life, and can be terribly annoyed and upset when these are disturbed.

As adults, we can also be more our own masters in creating or breaking rhythms to suit ourselves. We have the life experience and perspectives to deal with the regular and irregular occurrences. Children, on the other hand, are not at a point of having the perspectives on life enabling them to see the irregularities. Therefore they feel so much more secure in being able to anticipate that which comes to them, predictably and regularly.

A Question of Trust in the World

Many parents proudly proclaim that their 'kid' can adjust to anything. They make a virtue out of the fact that whatever they want to do and whenever and wherever they may want to go, their child is able to be with them. Their spontaneity has not been altered or hindered by the child. There is no doubt that children are very adaptable, but at what cost? We can grow callouses on the hands or on the soul and can withstand many unusual things. Have you ever watched a chef in a large, commercial kitchen handle pots of hot food without burning himself? Well, he has developed scar tissue and callouses that allow him to handle the great heat without being painfully sensitive, but at the same time he can hardly feel the difference between silk and course wool because his fingers have lost their sensitivity. The point is one of adjustment. We can adjust to many things but always at a price. For the child to adjust to the unrhythmic world of 'spontaneous' parents may mean that there is a lessened inner security and that the child's own rhythmical system is later on less strong than it could be.

A further step into the quality of time is the question of ritual and celebration. It isn't enough to progress from winter to spring, to summer and then fall in a rhythmic way; to be <u>conscious</u> of these changes is also very important. In ancient times, all important events were celebrated with some ritual observance. In that way, its importance could be recognized by all (the Gods and the people). Whether it was the course of the year, or the important stages of human life, each had its important celebration carried out in a ritualistic way.

Nowadays, we tend to consider most ritual celebrations as being either 'old-fashioned or 'religious;' many adults are put off or embarrassed by them. It is so difficult for us to fully enter into a ritual with our whole being because we want to be observer rather than participant. We are too self-conscious to fully participate. It is safer for most of us to hold back and observe but not lose ourself in the process. Children can still do that and benefit from the oneness and completeness of full participation. Even secular rituals such as high school and college graduations have been boycotted, ignored, or watered down so that there is hardly a feeling of meaningful celebration left.

Rituals have much to do
with tradition and
the work towards
gradually building
a rich tapestry of warm
colors and forms interwoven
with the shared experiences
of people. There is a nourishment
in tradition that stems from the feeling
of having done it before and being able to fit
into a process that is continuous, that has some
permanence and stability; that roots one in time and
space.

In our iconoclastic times, society has tended to become
distrustful of form, pattern, tradition, ritual: the
old. We have looked to the present and future rather
than to the past (except with distrust for its having
created the chaos and difficulty of the present). This
has enabled us to find our own way in this very new
world that has been changing at a rate far more
dramatically than ever before.

The challenge we face now is to create new and
meaningful rituals, celebrations and traditions which
need not be completely unchanging, but which do, at
least, have some form and substance. It has been almost
amusing (if it weren't so inwardly sad) to see how, as
we overthrow old traditions, new ones actually do arise
in their place - even though they may be somewhat devoid
of any real substance. Certain television programs have
become a focal point in many households, anticipated and
planned for; having taken on the elements of a cult. The
obvious problem is that it is focused on a non-human
activity (television), where there is little or no real

social interaction except on the lowest common level.

Within the family structure, ritual has been defined by sociologists as "that part of family life that the family likes about itself, is proud of and wants formally to continue."[6] The development of rituals by a family is like an index of the common interests of its members. And all too often we see that families in crises have very few shared rituals and hence few meaningful experiences that they hold in common. This makes life rather bleak and empty.

Rituals, when they are overdone, can make life somewhat static and encumbered; one may feel stifled by unchanging patterns and rhythms of life where each next step is prescribed in a certain and specific way. Yet children and adults do look back on the way things were done, and if pleasing, meaningful and good, they tend to want to respect and perhaps recapture that goodness. Most of us can think back to the favorite things, activities and foods that we have experienced and few of us would say: "I never want that again." We can all remember those special holiday times when the family gathered and there was a warm feeling of belonging to a 'special' group who did things in a 'special way'. That is a family experience.

Barbara Jackson, in a newsletter of the Sacramento
Waldorf School, describes her family Christmas as a kind
of memorable event about which we are speaking:

"Christmas dinner at Grandmother's house was a
magical time for us. It lifted us out of our
everyday selves as secretary, student, salesman,
nurse and teacher into the more elegant world of our
family's past. The great mahogany table with its
stiffly-ironed cloth filled the tiny diningroom. Its
top glittered and gleamed with the family treasure:
Great-Grandmother Manchester's monogrammed crystal,
mellow old silverware, and the good China, all
brought from England in the 19th century.

Our menu also came from England, and I suspect it
was older than the silverware. The meal centered
around the Christmas Pie - a huge beef roast which
was baked for hours in a soft crust made of suet and
flour. The Pie was served in big spoonfuls and
topped with a thin gravy. Most of the side dishes
were boiled: boiled potatoes, boiled onions, boiled
beans, and one time - boiled cabbage! Cranberry
sauce, homemade rolls and relishes completed the
meal, which was followed immediately be mince pie,
cheese and coffee.

After dinner, the men went out into the snow to
smoke, and every female over the age of 5 joined in
the dishwashing. Those were wonderful, steamy, jolly
hours we spent washing the good China and putting it
away for another year."

One might well ask what has happened to many of the
simple family rituals such as shared meals, a special
Sunday dinner, or that wonderful evening story to which

44

all would listen. Family rituals are those regular and dependable happenings which can give to each member of the family a sense of belonging to a home instead of just living in it. Ritual, celebration and tradition become the power that can create family unity and meaning far more than any material possessions.

As we well know, some of the most beautiful expressions of family life have come from the poorest families where there was the warmth, love and concern that nurtured the members, both young and old. Some of the most sterile childhood experiences are recalled by people who have had the 'silver spoon,' but lacked the real stuff of family which is the warm activity and feeling in which all partake.

It is of the utmost importance to remember that as parents we are not only doing things for our children, but that we are sharing experiences. In other words we share our life, our beings, our selves. If we stand outside the activities and pat ourselves on the back because we are so good to be doing this or that, or getting and giving this or that, then we are doing a disservice to all, and especially to ourselves. We need to come to the point of realizing that what we do within the family _is_ life and is as important as anything else undertaken in life. It should not be an obligation, but something that becomes rich, meaningful and wanted by all.

This be a particularly important idea for fathers to ponder as they are often a bit slower and more reticent in making that adjustment from their job in the 'outside' world to their life at home. How essential it is to give up the stand-offishness and to enter directly into the give and take of the family process, becoming part of the rituals and activity of the household. Bennett Olshaker, in his book The Child as a Work of Art [7] has a wise bit of advise: "What we really need for the sake of our children is an adequate quantity of quality time together."

That means sufficient time to be with the family and to really be there with one's whole being. It can also mean making the time we spend together of sufficient quality to improve the quality of our entire life. We need to choose quality activities that are meaningful and wholesome where we may all grow from and through the sharing.

Dr. Olshaker quotes Coleman McCarthy, a columnist for the Washington Post, who wrote of having taken his three young children to Florida for Christmas vacation so that his wife could have some leisure time at home. At the end of the trying week he was ready to get back to the relative peace and safety of his busy newspaper office. He ended his column with "but there was a new sensation in being with the boys..., and not many feelings of accomplishment have ever been fuller. It is strange how hotly so many men say they are seeking fulfillment in their work. Usually never getting there, but worse, never understanding that they might find it deeply and lastingly in sharing their lives a little bit more with their children."[8]

In recent years many fathers have re-entered the home in a meaningful way. In part it is because many mothers are working outside the home and responsibilities have been more evenly shared. There is also a rising number of families where the wife works outside and the husband is primarily in the home. Some men are finding that their lives are profoundly changed by reorienting their lives away from the "Hero's Quest" outside the home to the more inward and intimate journey of intense personal relationship.

Men have suffered terribly in our culture by having been given the image and role of outward Hero. Men have been taught from early age to value things (machines, cars, tools) and accomplishments (winning, scoring, beating out competitors) more than to value relationship, intimacy, feelings and processes. It is very difficult in marriage to reverse these values and take time and interest in the subtleties of children and family and the complex needs generated in the intensity of related and interdependent beings.

If we have been taught that all problems can be solved, i.e. broken engines can be fixed or replaced, trying harder will give us greater success, we, as men, become easily frustrated, confused and angry in situations where these are no easy answers. And often there are no easy answers in intimate family relationships. No winners and losers. Instead there is process, on going process which involves open and careful listening, sharing of vulnerability and realizing that the give and take is never ending.

The old patriarchal forms of structure and authority no longer work as well and men are being forced into a time of painful transition. Old roles are being challenged as are the old attitudes. Father no longer knows best and even if he does he needs to find better ways to express himself.

We come back now to the quantity and quality of time and what that can mean to our children and to us. Sufficient time needs to be spent with children in a relaxed, non-demanding way: hence sufficient quantity of 'quality' time where we are really fully present with our whole being; listening, talking, interacting and playing. Beyond that, we have the recognition of 'special' moments of time in rituals and celebrations shared by the family members which are repeated rhythmically. These 'special moments' are the center points guiding the wheel of life which goes forward at a steady pace, but which also goes in cycles and can be anticipated and relied upon to give stability to our lives.

Time becomes ever more complex. It can either weigh as a burden because we lose it, fight it, or are afraid of it, or it can be our ally because we live into it and flow with it and use it properly.

The next section will offer
some ideas and practical
suggestions on ways of
using, celebrating and
living with time,
rhythm and
ritual.

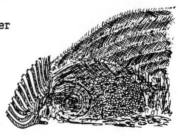

Living in Time

The Day

The day is the basic unit of time. The passage of
the sun from its soft, gentle lighting of the
eastern sky to its often dramatic, fiery exit on the
western horizon, marks the natural, basic unit of
time in which we all exist. Day, night and day again.
Light, darkness and light once more form the building
stones of time as we progress through life.

Each day brings us something new and unborn - new
challenges, new expectations, new dimensions in which
live the possibility of fulfillment and growth. The
cleansing and healing of the night provides us with the
strength to go forward. Having absorbed the lessons of
yesterday, we are hopefully better able to face today so
that tomorrow will be even more fulfilling.

We can really live only in the present. We may remember
yesterday and anticipate tomorrow but we are here, now.
Viewed in this way, each day calls for celebration
because it is unique, never to be experienced again.

Seconds, minutes and hours are our human creations: we tend to rush and cramp our lives to fit into this mechanical aspect of time. It is all too easy to go from one day to the next or from one hour to the next simply fulfilling our obligations, rather than taking that moment for real consciousness and celebration which gives meaning to life.

Before saying anything about what may be done with the family in celebration, a word should be said about how one may use some time alone in a constructive way.

Most of us are pulled in many directions with so many responsibilities, that it is often difficult to truly find our own center. Mother, wife, friend, daughter; or father, husband, friend, son are some of the many roles we play in relation to the world around us. Unless we are deriving strength and sustenance from an inner core of selfhood, we may overlook who we really are. In order to meet ourselves as we would a loved one, we have to be in touch with ourselves on a regular basis. Daily contact with ourselves is a must. It may sound easy and obvious, but the fact of the matter is, that in our lives it can sometimes be a most challenging problem to have or find the time to meet 'with ourselves' for a few moments.

We often use the expression: 'getting out on the wrong side of the bed' as an excuse for our bad temper during the day. This need not happen if we prepare ourselves to enter or re-enter our body after our experience in sleep.

To awaken in the morning just a few minutes before you

absolutely must and to use that time quietly and
constructively, can make all the difference to how a day
may go from there.

Contemplation Exercise

Upon awakening quietly contemplate: "I thank
the spiritual world which has held and
nurtured my soul and my consciousness while
the earth has guarded and looked after my
physical body. I recognize that during the
hours of sleep I haven't been in conscious
control of my being; rather I have been held
by forces and powers other than those I can
grasp with my day waking intellect. During
this time my physical body has recuperated
from the previous day's exertions and my
psyche (soul) is also refreshed. The healing
balm of the night's sleep has allowed me the
strength to now enter the new day."

During this quiet time, allow the feelings, thoughts and
a sense of direction of the day to come fresh from your
spiritual journey in sleep. In other words, the moments
just as we awaken are very special; as they are a
transition between the two great realms within which we
live: the spiritual and the earthly. Is it possible for
us to bridge these two worlds? Yes, but it takes an
inner effort, a consistent and conscious effort that may
take years until we see the fruits of our labours.[9] By
being inwardly still and attentive, we can sometimes

receive at least a sense of some of the directions we need to take and answers to some of the questions that we may have asked upon going to sleep. The old expression, 'Let me sleep on it,' comes out of the recognition that a 'higher' wisdom is just as much a part of us as our best everyday thinking.

This is an excellent time to pause and imagine what the day will bring. What are the major challenges facing us? What needs to be accomplished and most of all, what may be learned from this day to come?

Over the long term, it is very helpful to try picturing the day to come and in the evening to think back, matching the early morning picture against what actually happened. In time, we may find that the two grow to be more similar

All of this time spent alone need not be more than three to five minutes - but it can put us in a right frame of mind to face the day with all its joys, responsibilities and challenges. In a sense it is a gathering up of seeds, a harvest of the healing forces of the night.

Dreams

Are we attentive to our dreams? Do we take seriously the images that are presented to us from other levels of consciousness in which we live? Do we realize that dreams are like doors and windows to the spiritual world (the unconscious - in contemporary psychological terms).

The world out of which dreams come; an other level of our consciousness is a world of pictures and images.

Logic, rationality, space and time are left behind as we enter the unconscious. It is a magical and mythological world which no longer needs the physical substantiality which limits imagination in our every day "real" world.

Yet it is also a real world; one which operates by different laws and rules. Its language is that of image, symbol, metaphor, picture and myth. It is more real than the everyday sense perceptual world because it is related to the world archetypes (the images of universal truths) and the structures behind the physical world.

When we dream, our personal unconscious (and sometimes the more general world unconscious) speaks to us in this picture language which is laden with symbols. We see aspects of ourselves and the challenges we face. By no means is it easy to understand these images but they present themselves to us for a reason. Carl Jung suggested that dreams are an opportunity for us to see ourselves and what we need to be doing in relation to our inner being. The dream image is a gift of the gods and if we ignore it then the gods will insist that we learn our lessons even more dramatically. Illness, accidents, misfortune, crises are ways of learning some of the hard lessons of life. Dreams, if we are able to be attentive to them, are often letting us know what we need to do.

Of course learning to understand our dreams is no easy matter and often involves working with some one else who has the training and experience to help guide you into a healthy relationship with the material that is presented.

53

Our next deed, before emerging from bed, is for husband and wife to spend a few moments, after their private, individual time, looking at _their_ day. To share, still in the quiet and intimate mood, their dreams, how they slept, what they see happening in the day, what help they may need from each other and, what expectations they may have for themselves, for each other, their children, their work and so on.

This kind of sharing and inner touching can make all the difference in the mood of the day to come, for one of the great dangers and pitfalls of any relationship is assuming one knows what the other is thinking and feeling. These few moments give the opportunity to get beyond the assumptions and guesses and to genuinely touch the inner life of our mate. This isn't the time for long discussions, detailed planning and perhaps disagreements, but if handled well, it is the time to set directions, have a sense of common purpose and action and feel the support and consciousness of each other as the day begins. We should also have a moment to feel and express the emotional bond - the love - to and from the other person.

How can this be done on Monday morning when there is such a rush to get the children off to school and also not be late for work? The whole process from awakening to actually getting up and moving may take no more than ten minutes. Being up ten minutes earlier to get the day started in a peaceful, sane way is worth more than a few extra moments of fitful sleep which will soon be shattered by the rushing, bustling surge of activity.

and then the children

The next thing to be done is the awakening of children. The variations on this theme are as varied as children and their patterns. In cases where the parents actually awaken the children, it should be done gently and with a cheerful and yet reverent mood. Remember that at this moment you are bringing the children away from their stay with the healing forces of the heavens. A gentle song can set the tone of the new day. (It really doesn't matter whether or not you have a good voice or that you can sing in tune or not. What does count is that the children hear your voice and sense your devotion and love to what you are doing.)

Sitting on the bed, having opened the curtains, softly singing and holding your child allows for the "reentry" in a soft, loving way. A moment can be taken for asking about how he or she slept and what dreams were experienced. Then a sharing of what is happening that day, while perhaps the clothes are selected and the chores of washing, etc. are begun. Of course, depending on the age of the child, that routine will be modified, but what is important and perhaps universal is the touching, the talking and sharing, and the child's anticipation of that simple ritual on most mornings.

A cautionary word about rituals or anything rhythmic that we might want to do. It is very difficult to keep up any routine! We can usually start off with great enthusiasm the first day and perhaps the second day. Then something happens to prevent us doing it the third day and by the fourth day we have forgotten about it, or are discouraged. The only way is to persevere with love, devotion, and a sense of humour, knowing that as we begin something that has worth and value, we will also be tested in our resolve. It is this resolve and strongly motivated good will which will enable us to see anything through. It calls upon us to be conscious and strong and also to be tolerant about our own shortcomings. No matter, that we have forgotten! No matter that we are, at first inconsistent. The simple solution is to recognize the newness of each day and to begin again.

Meal Times

Meal times are one of the most important times for the family to come together. Every meal should begin with a grace which is a way of saying 'thank you' for the food that we eat. We don't have to be religious to say grace, for thanks can be expressed to God or to the forces of nature or to the people who have brought us the food. How exciting, even awe-inspiring to reflect on the mystery and wonder of how the food that is before us has come into being. Having started as a seed which was planted, nurtured and cared for, harvested, processed and, through an incredible number of steps, finally brought to our table. If that doesn't fill us with a feeling of awe and reverence for the world of nature and the endeavors of fellow human beings -- what will?

The two following graces are old favorites which are simple and profound:

Earth who gave to us this food.
Sun who made it ripe and good.
Sun above,
And Earth below
Our loving thanks
To you we show.

In the darkness of earth the seeds are awakened,
In the power of air the plants are quickened,
In the might of the sun the fruits are ripened.

In the shrine of the heart the soul is awakened,
In the light of the world the spirit is quickened,
In the glory of God man's powers are ripened. [10]

Following the saying of grace some families take hands around the table and say "Blessings on the meal." This simple, rhythmic act of joining, grounds the whole experience, especially for young children. The touching, the rhythm, the group activity, all make the experience live, not only in the head, but in the heart and hands as well.

What I have observed in countless families with small children is that once the routine of a grace before meals is started, which includes the children meaningfully, it will be the children who will remind the adults to "say grace" before beginning to eat. It is important to remember that verses such as the ones offered above, which everyone can say together, and the taking of hands has a rhythm, a meaning and an appeal that the more traditional free form, often rambling, "thanking of God" seems to lack.

Dinner

The evening meal should, whenever possible, be a time of sharing and should be taken together, as a whole family. If a family is a social unit then the rituals as a small society need to be honored, repeated and practiced regularly. "Breaking bread" is a sacrament in many religious traditions and it has power and strength on the archetypal level. It is, on that level, the act of transformation of the natural world, of the outer substance into the inner nutrition. There is a wonderful mystery around this process. In order for any food to be utilized by the body the digestive system needs to completely destroy the original substance which is foreign and threatening, and transform it into a "friendly" substance which may magically be absorbed into the body through osmosis. It is around this great alchemical transformation, this deep mystery of destruction of form and matter so that life may be sustained, that lies below the surface of each meal we eat. Simply lighting a candle at dinner time is an effective and meaningful deed which makes the statement that the evening meal is an important event. The meal eaten together is, in fact, a communion, a coming together, a breaking of bread, a sharing of effort and a time to be together. This is the coming together after the family has had its day's activity in various places and it is a time to share and exchange experiences. When possible the mood should be relaxed and light, providing the time for social communication where each member has a chance to share important and interesting events with the others.

Mealtime is a very important time of socialization for children of all ages. Table manners such as using utensils properly and the social graces of waiting until everyone is served before starting to eat, saying please and thank you, listening to each person in turn and offering food to others bespeak traditions of culture and heritage which have a worthy form. Each culture and civilization has its own ways but I find that far too many children now have few of these traditional ways which further alienate them from their own culture.

Of course, there are times when it is important for husband and wife to have a meal as a more intimate, adult experience. These times should not be overlooked as they can bring important moments of rekindling love, support and a feeling of closeness. And these are times when the stress and strain of busy lives dictate that the intimate time may be more important to the parents as people than picking up spilled peas and carrots off the floor. The caution flag goes up when the adults are eating alone more often than with the whole family.

Bedtime.

Bedtime is one of the most important times of the day for children. It will vary with their age but there are some general ideas that are universal.

The time of going to sleep should be as consistent as possible. This is part of the whole rhythmic structure in which the child feels comfortable. Early bedtimes are healthy for the child and for the parents. For the child, it is good because sleep is needed for healthy growth; for the parent, because it is important to have time as adults to do the reading, talking and socializing that is essential to one's own growth as an individual. Children who know that they have a regular bedtime and routine, go to bed and sleep much more easily than children who are left to determine their own time and who then regularly struggle, becoming over-tired and irritable.

Children on a regular schedule are far less prone to crying and fussing, and will be much less tyrannical and demanding because the limits have been clearly and lovingly established.

Tyrants

I would like to explore this idea of tyranny or the "Child as Tyrant" at this point so that it will throw light on much that will follow: we have all seen children, even very young ones who can be like absolute tyrants at times. I would suggest that in general those who are tyrants are usually those who have first been victims, who have been hurt psychologically at a deep level and who respond to the hurt and abuse with the defensive mechanism of being a tyrant. Why a tyrant?

A tyrant establishes some control over the surrounding

environment and by establishing this control creates boundaries and defenses so that the original abuse may stop. At a deeper level, the hurts and abuses may now at least be rationalized, an excuse given, for the punishments and hurts that may even still occur.

So, the tyrant develops ways of control. For a child it may be throwing tantrums, whining or any number of modes of behavior which will deflect or refocus the energy.

One of the great fears of children is that of the unknown. If bedtimes or mealtimes are not regular, are unknown, young children's responses may vary but the fussing, crying and whining are an unconscious way of gaining control of an insecure environment. Children need to feel trust in the environment and if there is not enough security they will try and regularize it by their own doing.

This idea of the tyrant, of course, can be carried into physically and emotionally abusive situations. Children who are hit and yelled at, often become tyrants as a way of fighting back. The irregular, irrational and threatening world created by the adult's irrational yelling and hitting, or the irregularity of basic needs for the child such as food, sleep, changing diapers all have a similar effect; to want, some how, to gain some measure of control, by whatever means possible.

Parents control the environment in which children live. The family, in fact, is an act of creation and we as parents are the authors, the creators of this work of art. It is a work of art, or can be, if we create with an aesthetic sense. Beauty as the ancient Greeks saw it had much to do with harmony. And what the Greeks hated and feared most of all was chaos, lack of form and order. The Greeks saw that the creative spirits made the heavens and the earth within a harmonic framework. I would suggest that children unconsciously crave that harmony in their surrounding. If it is there then the world is a place that can be trusted and in which there is security.

This is not sentimental or soft. In fact, we do not need to worry about the hard world of competition and unfriendliness until much later in life. Preparing children for the so-called "real" world very early in life does nothing more than make young people hard and cynical. Our challenge in families is to create a truly therapeutic, healing environment and the rhythm, regularity and ritual allows our children to relax in trust so that the unconscious work of childhood may continue rather than the child needing to compensate and protect itself from a harsh world prematurely. Children who feel secure, nurtured and honored do not need to be tyrants.

It is very difficult for many adults to find the profound in the simple. Children generally want the simple, the regular and the expected. They want life to be predictable and hence seldom tire of the same story told over and over again. We as adults have difficulty with this regularity and predictability and it is within this cosmos (the Greek word for harmony) of the family, we create, that we have the possibility to heal ourselves with the profound secret of simplicity. We have the possibility to be like little children again with awe and wonder at the little things. Most of all, by setting limits around the family, by creating a predictable and secure world we and our children can avoid the high price we all pay when the victim becomes tyrant in order desperately to gain some control over the environment.

Back to Bedtime

The basic elements of a bedtime routine for children up to the age of about twelve should include some quiet time spent with a story, perhaps some song and an evening prayer or verse. The story is a very special event. It may, at the earlier ages, be the reciting of simple nursery rhymes with some finger games and play. By the age of three to three-and-a-half, it should have evolved to the telling of simple stories, some of which should be <u>told</u> without the aid of a book. Simple experiences of nature and the seasons and the telling of "When I was little...". Children love to hear about their parents' lives and adventures and can hear the same story over and over again. Never be afraid to repeat stories to young children as they crave the familiar.

For older children, reading fairy tales, adventure stories, and good children's literature opens vast vistas for choice. (More detail is given in the section on literature.)

With young children especially, some songs are to be highly recommended. It doesn't matter how well we sing, we just need to sing with our children. There are many wonderful children's songs, folk songs and simple melodies available and children are soothed and nourished by this activity. It is only a matter of singing one or two songs - but that can make a world of difference in creating a special bond that revolves around sharing and expressing. In fact, the point to be emphasized about singing, as well as reciting nursery rhymes or telling stories is that not only are our children nourished by the content of the stories and relaxed by the activity, they feel secure in the shared experience. Also, there is the gradual appreciation of the parent as role model in two ways: First that their parent loves them enough to take the time to share with them - creating an intimate bond and secondly that their parent is creative, a creator, an author, an authority. When our children experience us singing songs, reciting verses and poems and telling (not reading) stories, they begin to sense that within an adult there is a wellspring running deep, out of which come wonderful treasures of the soul. Our jewels, our treasures sparkle in our children's eyes and delight their ears and nourish their souls. We become not only physical providers, but providers of soul content.

Children who experience depth in their parents, sense their authority not only on the physical, material level but as teachers. As parents we are called upon to be providers, teachers, role models and because of our own upbringing it may take extra work on our part to learn and know some of the things we want to share with our children, and it opens up new worlds to ourselves.

When we were children we did not experience this aspect of parenting. We feel unprepared, self conscious, incompetent. No one has taught us how to do these things. We are awkward, bumbling and shy. Yet our children, if they were to be critical, would not fault us for our efforts. Rather we will stand judged for not having tried; for not having nourished the imaginal life. As parents we have the opportunity to redo, reexperience our less than perfect childhood. We are called upon to find the little, unnourished child within us and to heal ourselves by painfully seeking our own creative source.

Interestingly, the more we try and the more we do, the easier it is to connect with the world of image and imagination. And our children love and appreciate us all the more for our efforts.

Children, especially young children learn by imitation. If we want our children to be creative, to take risks, to play; we need to set that example. And we will make mistakes and fall on our face from time to time but it is the effort and the courage to be vulnerable, to explore ourselves that creates the deep bond between parent and child.

Putting on a record, reading a book gives children the message that "other people" entertain us and that we can be passive recipients; observers of the world.
When children see and experience Mom and Dad singing, telling stories, playing games and daring to create, the message is that the creative source lives in each one of us. It is not some distant, alien thing. We have the power to be!

Candles, Prayers and Good Night

The lighting of a candle and the saying of a verse
as the last thing before saying good night creates
that special mood of quiet so that the child may
enter the world of sleep in an opened and relaxed way.
It is a simple ritual and whoever has experienced
candle light in a darkened room can surely
recall the magic of the flickering light
and the rainbow-like halo around the
flame. And it is that special
light which signals to
the child that the
end of the day
has come.
In this magic
moment of the
candle time
the transition
from the day
world to
the dream
world is
happening.
When this
is done
regularly with,
what I would call,
a religious devotion,
children sense that
the lighted candle
becomes the limit, the
boundary between waking
and sleeping and generally
go right to sleep.

A wonderful prayer that I have used for my children follows. It was at first simply said for the children. Gradually as they grew older they joined in and said it too.

From my head to my feet
I am the image of God.
From my heart to my hands
His own breath do I feel.
When I speak with my mouth
I follow God's will.
When I see and know God
In mother and father,
In all loving people,
In the trees and the flowers,
In the birds, beasts and stones,
Then no fear shall I feel
Only love will then fill me
For all that is around me, here.[11]

In this verse lives a simple and yet complete picture of the human being and our connection to the world around us. We are not praying <u>for</u> something or to something. We are simply giving an imagination, a picture of the single individual and the world and connecting the child to the creative spirits.

It may be important here to distinguish between prayer in the usual sense and what I have called verses. In the above example the verse gives an image. It is similar to a piece of poetry with its carefully organized use of words and rhythmic sounds woven together to form an image. It asks for nothing other than for one to "see" the picture. Prayer often is asking for something from

God or a supreme being. We want the gods to "hear" us, to acknowledge us, to protect us or bless us with some gift. There are certainly times for one or the other. My preference especially with small children is not to ask anything from God but to simply live in the image which in the long run gives children a sense of security without making them cynical and disappointed when what they ask for doesn't happen.

The Heart of the Family Day

Many people work outside the home in addition to having the responsibilities of parenting. The few intensive hours between five and eight PM, when we are together with our children, follow our own long day of work. These evening hours with the children are most important for them and we should try to enter that time sequence as fully as possible. That means, to not carry over our frustrations, anger, and annoyances from the job allowing them to spill into the children's time. This takes a great effort of will to temporarily postpone or put aside the work-a-day world and its effects on us for those several hours so that we can enjoy, be nourished by and be nourishing to our children.

Appearing to be involved with the children but really still inwardly churning, mulling, fuming and reliving the work day, is dishonest and is usually sensed by the children who will react in any number of ways. Crying, nagging, demanding are a few of the alternatives; but for many children it may be a far more subtle resentment that builds with time. Because children are naturally closer to the world of the unconscious, to the psyche, they are even more sensitive to our lack of soul honesty than we may think. Often the difference is simply that children are less able to verbally articulate what is going on for them or what they may be sensing or feeling. But they are affected by what goes on in our unconscious, in the inner world of the adults around them. And if we are not true to ourselves children will find a way to awaken the family by acting out, (rather than speaking out) so that something will happen.

Often in my counselling, I have experienced that a family which comes with a "difficult" child actually ends up being a family which is in need of much help. The "presenting problem", the child, actually has been like a lightning rod and draws attention, albeit negatively, to the fact that a lot of things are happening in the family below the surface and no one is dealing with them. Tensions between husband and wife, financial problems, issues that are unspoken, may affect the entire family system and the children become victims of the family wound. Often, as victim, they exert a negative power and hence become the tyrants of the family. (see page 60 on Tyrants)

In order that we not use our children as a dumping ground for our problems or that we are not being true to them, we need to be able to leave the world outside for a few hours and allow ourselves to be cleansed and healed by fully giving ourselves over to that time with the children. Here is what we might call the Heart of the Family Day. It is during this time, at least during the five days of the working week that we spend most of our time with our children. Mornings are usually a rush getting dressed, making breakfast and lunches and getting children off to day care or school and parents off to work. For most families it is not high quality time. We may all come home tired but we have also had experiences that may be shared. Some have been good and positive and others have been hard, and some rough edges may need smoothing.

Supper and chores need to be done and should be. So within this short three or four hours there is the possibility of much intense activity. Most of all there also needs to be time and attention given to play and solid, sincere human relating.

Adult Time

Once children are asleep, the family, whether it is husband and wife or a single parent should also have its own celebrations. Now with the children in bed comes the adult time. For the couple it should be a time of conversation and sharing as well as a time to enjoy each other's company. It is vitally important to know the other person, to be continually in-touch with all the struggles, the challenges, the successes and failures, the hopes and aspirations. A growing relationship demands that we be able to share from our inner core on an on-going basis.

Single Parents and All Parents as People

For the single parent, the sharing with oneself is vitally important. This is a bigger challenge and even more essential. To look at where you are, take stock, have a picture of the situation is to give yourself a meaningful, firm perspective.

A wonderful book called <u>Flying Solo</u> by Kenneth Wydro[12] gives many wise and insightful suggestions on dealing with the single experience. He points out that the key factors in centering one's life are each and every day self-determined and self-actualized deeds which come from within, activated by you, and no one else. This is a lesson for all, whether single or married.

Regular activities that become a part of your life provide ways of growing from within, whether they be a warm bath each evening where you can reflect on the day and see yourself objectively, or the keeping of a journal in which you can record your important thoughts, feelings and experiences. Activities which provide enjoyment as well as challenge and stimulation, such as learning a musical instrument, writing poetry, carving, sewing and so on, are vitally important. This is the stuff of life. It is, over the long term, what makes us greater than ourselves and more interesting to ourselves and to others. People who are absorbed in interests and activities are simply more interesting people.

It is usually the time, after the children are in bed, when we can celebrate ourselves and our own striving most intensely, whether we are single or married. We usually use the excuse that we are too tired and in fact we often are exhausted from our hectic lives by the time the children are in bed. What I am suggesting is that we gain nourishment and strength from having our own interests and our own activities. All too often we give out all during the day in our various roles as workers, parents, lovers and friends. Somehow we need to find ways of replenishing our own selves. That wellspring of creativity needs to be replenished by our own interests and activities that are meant for no one other than ourself. A good book we read may give us images that

71

nourish us during our days, and a poem we write or a picture we paint may also do the same. All too often we tend to choose the more passive activities so that we are entertained when actually a bit of extra effort will bear a sweeter fruit. Each day we should be able to take part in this continuing celebration of life both by our self and with our spouse.

Another point needs to be developed: Whether we live in relation to another or alone it is absolutely essential to develop self interests. The old "Jewish Mother" type lived her life for everyone else and when the children left the nest she had nothing and no one to live for. That was ultimately a hollow experience which in the end was negative for those around her. Her devotion to family members became less free and her family became stifled by guilt and the strings that were attached to each of her "good" deeds.

In order to be able to be a good spouse, parent, friend we each need to be loving, caring and attentive to our self. We can't give to others what we don't really have inside us. The hobbies, interests, pursuits that we ourselves undertake, make us more alive for those around us. The enthusiasm we may share, for what we are doing may light fires of enthusiasm in others and spank interest in mutual adventures of exploration.

Husband and wife will be closer and the relationship will be more soulful when each can come to the other brimming with their own enthusiasm rather than relying on our spouse to give us that excitement.

Also, it becomes hypocritical for us as parents to expect children to be exciting, interesting and interested when we are not. Children who come from homes

72

where parents read, read. Those who come from homes where parents have vital interests and activities also have vital interests and activities.

The Week

In the Biblical sense God created the heavens and the earth in six days and rested on the seventh day.
Our individual tasks are not quite as extensive as God's; work for most of us lasts five days with a rest period of two, and hopefully we are not trying to create the world each week. The week and the weekend are two cycles within the larger cycle of the seven day week. This seven day rhythm is universal and one that is and has been observed by most peoples throughout history.

In the old fashioned Jewish home, the Sabbath, Friday sundown to Saturday sundown, was a special time in many ways. The traditional Friday evening meal was the beginning of this time and was special, using the best china, a religious ritual and specially prepared food. There was never any mistaking that meal from any other in the course of the week. It stood out as a highlight of family ritual that was

73

practically inviolate within the scope of each person's relationship to the family.

For many traditional Christian homes the Sunday afternoon dinner, after church, was a special time of gathering. Many older people can look back to these gatherings with vivid, warm memories of aunts, uncles, grandparents gathering together and sharing a good time. These were times when it felt good to be part of a larger group, to belong, to listen, to learn about what others had to share. As children, we could look forward, with anticipation, to the event that would happen next week and remember what had happened the week before.

When we were growing up stores were closed after six p.m. and on Sundays. This provided a clear delineation between work and play/rest time. Nowadays, society and culture have blurred those once clear lines and it is up to us, individually, and as families, to create that rhythm which may be health giving in the course of a week.

For many young families, where there has been work and/or school during the week, the weekend becomes nothing more than a time to catch up on chores and to prepare for the week to come. The struggle is to find some time to break that "vicious circle" and create "creative" time.

Creative time for self and for family is a must. It may be going for a walk with the family, going to the zoo or a museum, making something such as a toy with the children or simply playing a game without worry about the time that is being spent in doing it.

Every weekend should have some 'special' event that is done as a family; something done for enjoyment where there is a shared experience. It might be 'spontaneous' or better yet, it might be planned in advance so that there can be a healthy anticipation in which all can participate. The important thing is that it is not done out of obligation; that it be a joyful experience which is really what we, in freedom, want to do, allowing ourselves to fully live it and then to think back upon it with a warm glow of memories. By joyful I do not mean frivolous or silly or simply some form of mindless fun. At times we may have this kind of fun but it is important to experience, at times, joyful as being full of meaning, interesting, informative and challenging.

In talking with my older children it has often surprised me that one or another has vivid memories of things that we did together a few times which over the years became translated into 'tradition.' "Didn't we take a drive into the country every Sunday?" The fact was that we did it occasionally. The point is that those adventures did make vivid impressions which were nourishing; leaving deep and lasting impressions in addition to the warm feelings of having shared 'special times' together.

There is a fine line to artfully choose the right experience or activity for children at particular ages that will also suit the entire family. When is a trip to the zoo or a museum appropriate? How long a ride should we take with our three year old? There are few right answers but what becomes important is to bring to experience, imaginally, what the inner world of our children is like. This is not an easy task and actually needs to be approached from two aspects.

Observing the Children

I am always amazed that most of us, as adults, have gone through the process of childhood, having experienced the various developmental stages of growth and development and yet we often forget that we have gone through these stages and that we are quite different now than we used to be.

Everyone of us starts as an embryo, is born and continues to grow in physical size and inner complexity. Not only are we different in size, but our intellectual, emotional and social needs and capacities are different at each stage of our life's journey. The way we perceive and experience the world changes as does how the world effects our inner and outer self.

The unfortunate thing I see today, along with the loss of instinct in the raising of children, is this huge loss of memory about how we are different than we were when we were younger. We no longer seem able to hold on to our own experiential truths of our childhood and to recognize the wonder, the awe, the innocence that was ours, at least until a certain point in our life. And if we do remember, acknowledge and perhaps honour that child-ish stage we tend to be ashamed of it or discount it in some way.

We might ask the question: Why or how have we forgotten something so basic in our lives? The answer to this is not easy nor could it be definitive but it is important to at least touch on a few aspects because of what can be learned about our society.

All of us are influenced, to some extent by theories and

ideologies that pervade our culture. These theories, which quickly become the foundations of our world view colour the way we see the phenomena of the world or even the way we see ourselves. Before Charles Darwin most people saw themselves as divine creations. After Darwin people began to see themselves as higher forms of animals and that rather than a divine origin we had somehow started off as accidents of the natural selection process. This has influenced the way western society sees itself and how it values such things as competition and survival.

Early in this century Freud presented several theories about human behavior which centered around the child's relation to the world of the parents. His Oedipal theory suggested that sons had an ambivalent relationship with their fathers because they loved their mothers and, at the same time loved and hated their fathers. The son was jealous of the father's sexual union with mother and inwardly struggled in competition with this powerful male figure of father until he could somehow overcome him.

Another aspect of Freud's view of childhood was that girls had sexual fantasies of their fathers so that when women spoke of incest and sexual abuse most of it was, in fact, only fantasy and had not actually happened.

These views have crept into the modern psyche to the extent that although developmental stages of growth and consciousness are acknowledged, we still ascribe to the mind of the child the sexual motives of the adult. This makes the child a little adult whose consciousness is basically the same. If sexuality is ascribed to the child we are intrinsically denying the preconscious and

77

less self conscious stages of awe, wonder and innocence.

When we look at the use of children as sex symbols in modern commercials we begin to fathom the logical extension of what has happened to the image of childhood in this century. Child sexual abuse, incest and the general sexualization of childhood are all shockingly on the rise. Parents throw up their hands in despair and teachers complain at the growing sophistication of children at ever earlier ages. And children are painfully caught in this web of projections which impose on their personalities from the outside instead of allowing the inner being to organically unfold. They are robbed of their childhood and thrust into adultness sexually, emotionally and intellectually all too early.

As parents we are faced with several problems which weave together. We have been brought up within the general world view that there is little difference between the consciousness of children and adults; this has been reinforced in magazines, books, and school to the point that most people hardly question it even though our felt experience may be different. This leads to a second thread which is that our own feelings, experiences and instincts are not valued, honoured or even believed. We distrust ourselves and take outer "authorities" to be more truthful and accurate. We lose confidence in ourselves; in our dreams, memories and feelings. Not much is left to give us confidence in what we have to offer so that we turn to the modern media for possible answers to basic life questions. Popular books, television and radio talkshows proliferate giving us the latest opinions. This sounds good and that sounds better and in a few months something else is presented that changes our views once more.

Rudolf Steiner, in keeping with his general approach to
life, often came back to the simple and yet challenging
suggestion that what was most needed was to relearn the
art of careful observation. If we want to really know
our children we need to put away our theories, ideas and
intellectualism and allow the phenomena (in this case
ourselves and our children) to speak for itself. If we
begin from an early age to carefully
observe our children and to use
our inner and outer eyes
we will see what our child's
real needs are. We will need
to continually check to see if it
is our child we are seeing or whether it is
something within us that is speaking loudly while
blocking out what our child is really presenting to us.

Many of us, by the time we come to adulthood have been
hurt in various ways. We have needs, we have defenses,
we have scars from our own upbringing, In many ways we
have been taught not to trust ourselves and we may have
parts of ourselves that are unnourished. How are we to
merge all this neediness from ourselves (much of it
unrecognized and unacknowledged) with our child who
comes to us with innocence and trust?

Obviously there is no easy and straight forward answer.
But perhaps we need to go back to that seemingly simple
suggestion to develop a way of consciously and
unselfishly observing the phenomena. In order to do this
we need to gradually realize what in us we bring to the
observed object; what are we projecting on to the other
that is really part of ourself. If we are engaged in
this process of checking and rechecking what is ourself
and what is the other, on an ongoing basis we have at

least started to take the first step at honouring the individual being of our spouse and/or child.

Many parents end up living out unfulfilled parts of themselves through their children. This is something that is done unconsciously and may have painful consequences on their children. A mother who wanted to be a dancer and gave up or was somehow thwarted along the way may see in her daughter a potential dancer who needs to be pushed, prodded and cajoled into dancing even though she does not really want to do so. The child is made to act out mother's needs and only later, with much pain and struggle is she able to break free of this. Mother wasn't malicious but she was unconscious of what was her own and what was her daughter's. The damage is done.

Many well meaning parents teach their children to read early so that they can get a head start in life. But a head start toward what? For whom? If we dig deeper we may find that the parents' own competitive nature, their own drivenness and will to succeed is pushed onto the young and receptive child. Early reading and other accomplishments on the part of the child reflect back on the parents who are the ones really needing the strokes that come with success. Often the child becomes part of this and soon there is a driven, competitive child in whom the parents may be very proud. At other times the child's own individuality may rebel at being pushed and so the child is seen as stubborn, slow or in some way unmotivated.

We often see the play instinct which is actually a sacred rite; an important aspect of exploring and learning the world twisted into the realm of organized sport. Children, especially before adolescence are wanting to play and they learn about life through creative play in which they can make the rules and live the life of the game. In sports we quickly find that the rigidity of the established rules, limited time, specialized equipment and particular skills and movements all go toward destroying the flexibility and creativity of the youngster. In sports there are winners and losers and successes and failures. Many parents think that learning to compete early in life will some how give their child an edge later in life. The fact of the matter is that often we see children who have been early competitors burnt out, cynical and disappointed; or, if they have adjusted to this way of relating to the world, they will be driven, competitive and always on the go to win one more event. The damage is done for the competition becomes far more important than cooperation and compassion. The world is viewed as being divided into winners and losers, good and bad, for and against. It is a bipolar world without the mediating force of heart. Of course much of the push on early childhood sports comes from parents who are acting out, through their children, unfulfilled aspects of themselves.

Choosing activities for children and for the family is very complex, indeed. What is it that my child really needs and what is it that I need and want.
Self observation (painful as it can often be at times) and the unfettered observation, the inner seeing and hearing of our children are the starting points.

81

The Festivals of the Year

Just as we live in the natural rhythm of the day and week, so too might we consider that the earth itself has a natural rhythm in the course of the year. This rhythm is like a great inbreathing and outbreathing which in its undulations, carries us forward unceasingly. There are obvious times of expansion and contraction. In our own breathing and pulse our lives have a steady rhythm of in and out, expansion and contraction. We can also see this rhythm of opposites in awakening and sleeping, in the course of the day. With the earth, there is also a rhythm of action and rest - expansion and contraction, light and dark, cold and hot.

The farmer knows this all too well, as does anyone living close to nature. For anyone sensitive to the course of the year, the difference in feeling and the varied experience of self also follows the seasons. We tend to feel more in-drawn and introspective during the depths of winter, while during summer, the strong forces of nature tend to pull us ever outward, uniting us with the forces of light and growth. 'Spring Fever' is not a mere coincidence, it reflects the transition from a more point-centered consciousness to the consciousness of the periphery.

Our own relationshiop to the course of the year and to nature is the heart of the matter. What we say about ecology, littering and conservation may be lovely, but what we do, how we take active responsibility for the world around us is what really matters. What we do, our deeds and actions, are real for ourselves and our children. We cannot survive for long just thinking about sleep or about breathing, we need to actually engage in doing them. So too with the rhythms of nature; we need to actively live in the course of the year in whatever ways we find possible in our particular circumstances.

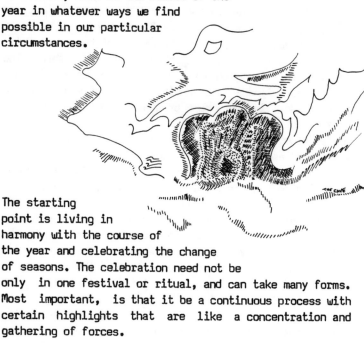

The starting point is living in harmony with the course of the year and celebrating the change of seasons. The celebration need not be only in one festival or ritual, and can take many forms. Most important, is that it be a continuous process with certain highlights that are like a concentration and gathering of forces.

Most great religions and cultures have recognized the great seasonal changes and have celebrated them in one way or another. We have the remnants of these celebrations; although all too often, they have tended to lose the original, inner meaning, becoming commercialized with greeting cards, presents and empty fluff. The individual challenge we face in modern society is to personalize and decommercialize the great festivals of the year, making them times of meaning through our conscious activity.

Looking at the Year

Starting with the Autumn season we have the gradual in-drawing of the forces of nature after the profusion of growth and blossoming of summer.

Outwardly, we see and experience the great bounty of fields and trees; harvests of vegetables, grains and fruits and then the gradual 'dying back' of natural forces. The sun's power grows weaker, the days grow shorter, a chill is felt in the air. In a way, the wonderful transformation of nature is reflected in the new colors to be found on the deciduous trees with their golden, orange, scarlet and brown leaves. The world of green, the predominant color of the plant kingdom, gives way to this rainbow of color, quite different from the light, delicate colors of spring or the bold, bright summer flowers. For anyone who has observed the changing seasons, there is a most wonderful progression from the light, delicate greens of spring, to the dark greens of summer to the golden fiery colors and finally to the browns of late autumn. This final burst of autumn color is, in reality, the ending of an era; a death, a signal that the forces of outer growth have come to an end. What we now see in the bare trees and fields is the skeleton of past growth and life which, at some time in the future, will be full of life and growth once again.

As we look at the scenes of nature during winter, we see the plant world at rest, seemingly asleep or dead. There is little activity or movement, little color except for the more somber tones of brown, greys and perhaps the pure white of snow.

... and the Day

Surely this is a metaphor for the course of each day that we live. The whole cycle of our awakening and sprouting in the morning, refreshed by sleep, to the activity of the day, hoping to be able to harvest the results of the day's activities, gradually going inward in the evening and finally to sleep where outwardly all is still and at rest. Then it takes eyes of another kind (insight) to see how the forces of health, restoration and regeneration are at work to prepare us during sleep for the next day to come.

The mystery of the rhythm of the human day and the greater 'day' of the earth and nature (the year) can call forth from us only a sense of awe and reverence for the world in which we have been placed. We live as a microcosm within the macrocosm; as the grain of sand within the universe. We reflect in our selves the rhythms of the year. We reflect in our very physical body the kingdoms of nature and the oceans of the world. No matter how much we may deny it we are the stuff and

85

essence of nature. We are the offspring of mother nature and have the living spirit within us.

Taking Time For

The first step in living with the course of the year and of being more in harmony with nature, is to become ever more conscious of nature. One simple way is to make sure that individually and as a family, some time is regularly set aside to observe that which is around us. Whether it be our own backyard, the local park or the trees on the street; just opening our eyes, ears and nostrils to what is around us, quickly brings an enthusiasm for the wondrous happenings of nature. To come home from work or shopping joyfully exclaiming "Have you seen the beautiful colors of the sunset tonight?" or "That old elm tree is just getting its new buds" will awaken in our children a desire to look and experience what we have just seen. To observe the clouds overhead and see a dragon or a horse riding in the sky can foster a new way of looking, filled with imagination that can easily set a child to hours of creative observation and increasing imagination.

Too many of us are so busy that we have little or no time to take a walk and look at the grass, flowers, trees and birds that are right nearby - even in the midst of a big and congested city. Activities as simple as this bring joy and health to ourselves and awaken something in our children that may well have lifelong benefits; becoming a 'love affair' with nature.

One activity that has proved very successful is to 'adopt' a tree or a small corner

of a garden or park and
to observe and get to
know it very well
through regular
visiting times.
Children are
amazingly observant
to every subtle change
over the course of time;
and how exciting it is to
make new discoveries as the
days, weeks and months pass.

A wonderful sense for past,   present and future can
develop when in winter we can remember how a bare tree
looked as its tiny green leaves first appeared, soon
growing larger, the light yellow-green color gradually
turning to a deeper and fuller green. Gradually in
autumn they turned to various colors; finally to a dull
brown as they fell to earth.

To collect twigs, leaves, flowers as 'treasures' from
nature and to have a prominent corner of the living room
or family room that shows a display appropriate to the
season, is one way to bring 'nature' into the home.
Abundant flowers in spring and summer or sprays of
autumn leaves in fall enhance the beauty and decor of
the home and stand as lively reminders of nature's
activities.

Even more important, are the various activities such as
planting seeds in the spring, whether in the garden or
back yard in suburbia or in a planter box in the city.
Even a three-year-old will take great joy in helping to
plant some seeds and if guided carefully can wait with
great anticipation for the young sprouts to peek through

87

the soil. Here is the very mystery of life and we enter and become one with the creative spirits; helpers to Mother Nature in this act of planting and tending to tiny seeds. So much of life's experience is death, destruction and interferring with nature so that it is invaluable for the yound child; for any child to engage in the birthing process of plants or animals.

Collecting colorful leaves, pressing and then sealing them with a warm iron between sheets of waxed paper, can create a beautiful display when hung in a window. Be creative and imaginative and find those activities best suited for your situation; don't be afraid to first experiment and then to repeat over several years what was once successful, as children love traditions and will look forward from year to year to do that 'special' activity at the same time next year.

For a number of years, we would drive out to the cherry orchard in mid-June and get boxes of ripe, delicious Bing cherries. The house would be full (as were our stomachs) of the fragrant sweetness as we preserved quart after quart of the cherries. With joy, in fall, winter and the next spring, we would have one of our favorite desserts and remember the 'cherry time' in June.

We all knew the rotation that then began in the warm Sacramento Valley. After the cherries came the apricots, plums, peaches and pears. We could eat our way around the garden, as one by one, the trees offered us their bountiful gifts. This was one, very tasty way of uniting with nature.

Spring

Our job as parents is to welcome our children to their home on earth and to guide them on their journey through life. Some of the great signposts along this time/space path are the seasonal festivals. In many ways, spring is the beginning of the new year. At least it is the awakening, from a visual point of view, of the cycle of nature. It is not quite true to say that in spring we see a birth of the forces of nature; more accurately, it is a rebirth; a time of resurrection; of passing over from the old and unseen to the visible. We can experience a time of the rising of our sap, as well as the sap in the trees. Here is levity - in action - as the forces of growth overcome the downward pull of gravity in the fall and winter.

In the Jewish tradition, it is the time of Passover, a celebration of the Angel of Death passing over the homes of the Jews who had annointed their door posts with the blood of the Paschal lamb. It was also the time of the rebirth of the Jewish people, who were then free to leave their slavery and bondage in Egypt and journey back to the promised land.

The symbolism of the Passover Seder (or meal) speaks eloquently of the meaning of a spring festival. The egg as the symbol of eternal life; the mystery of life contained within the perfection of the smooth protecting shell. The lamb, born in spring, showing the bountiful life that arises each year; the bitter horseradish and the sweet honey and apples as contrasts that humanity must experience as important aspects of life. The sacramental unleavened bread and wine are taken to cleanse and heal the body. The Seder becomes a meal and religious experience to be celebrated by the family which is the primal unit of human life.

In the Christian tradition of Easter, we see the betrayal of Christ, His crucifixion, death and resurrection; His being reborn into the spiritual world after an earthly death. It is, in the deepest and most spiritual sense, a true festival of the spring, for it speaks to us of rebirth on the highest level.

For the young child, spring should be a joyous celebration of Nature's rebirth. The Easter bunny bringing eggs, is really the symbol of the abundance of nature's regenerative powers, bringing
the seed of the new beginning.
It is not so much the
buying of chocolate
eggs and plastic
baskets, as
it is the
painting and
decorating of
eggs - together
as a family - and
the making of a simple
basket with the children
that leads to the active
participation and the
anticipation of the big event.
The Easter egg hunt should come with the sense that something very special has happened and that the Easter Bunny has found us, no matter where we happen to be. If we go out into nature (our backyard) we will find the mysteries of nature revealed to us. 'Seek and ye shall find!'

With any festival, rather than preaching about its meaning, or trying to give an intellectual lesson - a good story should be told. One of the best images which gives a true picture of the Easter or spring experience is the story of the butterfly.

In bare outline, which you should be able to embellish out of your own inner work and life experience, is a simple rendition:

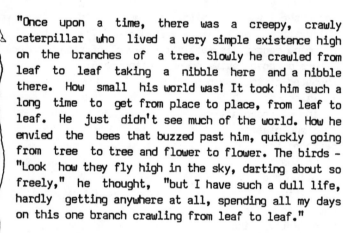

"Once upon a time, there was a creepy, crawly caterpillar who lived a very simple existence high on the branches of a tree. Slowly he crawled from leaf to leaf taking a nibble here and a nibble there. How small his world was! It took him such a long time to get from place to place, from leaf to leaf. He just didn't see much of the world. How he envied the bees that buzzed past him, quickly going from tree to tree and flower to flower. The birds - "Look how they fly high in the sky, darting about so freely," he thought, "but I have such a dull life, hardly getting anywhere at all, spending all my days on this one branch crawling from leaf to leaf."

One day as he crawled along he saw a butterfly with its delicate, beautifully iridescent wings. Oh, how he wished he could be so beautiful. The caterpillar laughed scornfully, "Look at me, with my long low body and many legs. How could I ever be like that?"

Time passed, and on a warm day with the sun shining brightly, the caterpillar was filled with a new urge. He needed to do something that he had never done before. Soon, he was weaving a house for himself out of a silky, fine thread which came from his body. No one had taught him how to do it - but yet, he knew just what to do. On and on he went, winding the fine thread around himself in a beautiful oval shape which looked like a soft white silken egg. After a while, he was fully enclosed. He curled up, not knowing what else to do, and fell into a long dream/sleep. Time passed and he was unaware of the changes which took place in his body. He didn't know that he lost his form; that he became a mass of cells floating in a soup whose recipe only Mother Nature knows.

Then came a day when there was a stirring within the cocoon and our little friend began to awaken. In this silken egg, bit by bit there were tiny cracks which grew bigger until, finally, the cocoon opened and a somewhat dazed little being emerged, feeling and looking very awkward and unsure. As the sun shone down upon him - strange to behold - wings began to unfurl. Our old friend, the caterpillar, who had entered the cocoon, now looked and felt quite different. No longer did he have all those little legs and the long fuzzy body. His beautiful iridescent wings slowly dried in the sunlight. A gentle puff of wind came along and he was sailing through the air, learning quickly how to use his new sense of freedom.

Briefly, the sight of a caterpillar slowly creeping along a leaf sparked a dim fleeting memory of his past. He flew on, high over the trees and then low to the ground trying to see all the world. He soon forgot his past and was excited only by the very moment in which he lived."

This little story is an image of transformation and metamorphosis, which is the basis of the Easter/spring experience of death and resurrection; of new life emerging from the old. No more need be said to a child. No great explanation need be given. The picture and the outer reality stand by themselves.

Once again, the details and the form chosen for the celebration of spring should come out of yourself. In that way, it will be more true and vital. In order that a seasonal celebration have substance, it must come from within, from each person's inner search. Be creative and enjoy the preparation and carrying out of the celebration. Here is your chance to be an artist.

Traditionally, the seasonal festivals are celebrated at the equinox or solstice which are astronomically determined points in the year. They signal the beginning of the season; in reality we are pointing the way to what is coming. The mood we create at this time is one that helps make the transition to the new season.

Summer

Looking at the mid-summer festival which occurs around June 21, is perhaps more difficult because, in our time, it is barely recognized except in passing, as the official beginning of the summer season. In ancient Celtic and Ukrainian traditions, for instance, it was considered a time of purification. On that day all hearth fires were extinguished; the hearths cleaned and new fires prepared. The new lighting came only after a large fire was started in the town square. Cattle and swine were driven through it and lads and lasses leapt the fire; cleansing by fire on the longest day of the year, when the sun is at its highest point, having its most direct connection with the earth. So from the great source of light, life and warmth above, at its moment of greatest impact, we cleanse and renew, relighting our fires, giving ourselves to the forces of outer life and light.

As spring is the time of rebirth and new growth, summer

is the time of life at its fullest, outer light at its brightest. Here we have the possibility of nature's growth toward outer maturity. It is a time of fullness and of living in and with those forces of nature that in summer are so very strong.

My family has celebrated this festival with others in our community and has seen it done in other places, beginning with a family or group picnic followed with games, swimming and fun filled activities including singing and square dancing. As the sun began to set, we would gather to sing and to give praise to its mighty power. With its faint rays crossing the skies, we gathered around the large bonfire watching it blaze in startling brilliance. We could feel its heat and catch the warm glow of the sparkling flames. More songs (there are many old songs to be found exulting in the mid-summer mood), and as we formed a large circle around the fire, we created a periphery around the light filled center. As the fire burned down, the more adventurous in the circle jumped the fire to cheers of encouragement from the others.

Autumn.

The fall festival is also one which is hardly known today except perhaps through the national holiday of Thanksgiving, celebrated later in the season than it really should be. (Although in many ways, it does capture a real mood of the harvest festival.) The end of September, when the fall equinox actually occurs, would be a better time, but we live in this society and should respect its traditions, lending meaning to them where we can. The only thing more that should be said about Thanksgiving, is that in addition to making that fine traditional meal, we ought to take the time to tell the story of the holiday and bring meaning to a ritualistic meal instead of just satisfying ourselves with the delicious stuffed turkey.

Returning to the time of the autumn equinox, we do find in many older traditions, the celebration of Michaelmas - the festival of Saint Michael. Saint Michael is not really a saint, but rather in Hebrew and Christian traditions an archangel who stands on the right hand of God, serving the Spirit of the times. Michael is portrayed in art as a warrior with either a shining sword or a spear raised and pointed at a dragon, in the act of subduing it rather than actually killing it. That is left to others. Each one of us has the challenge of conquering our own dragon or demon.

Who is this dragon that needs to be overcome, slain or at least subdued? It is the so-called 'lower' element in us (sometimes called our shadow) that sets up the challenges that we each face in life; it may be our weaknesses or even our strengths that have gotten the best of us. In western traditions, the dragon has stood for power, brute strength, and sometimes cleverness in an earthly, amoral, grasping and greedy sense. It originates in the nature forces, outside and within us that have not been transformed by higher knowledge, a sense for the spiritual world or a purpose beyond the gratification of the lower self. The dragon is always hungry for more food, wealth, power and so on. It lives in the sulfurous, dark, hot, steaming recesses of confusion and unclarity or unconsciousness. Saint Michael, wielding the clear, gleaming sword or spear (which in mythology has symbolically stood for higher powers and revealed knowledge) stands as an adversary of the dragon by pushing down the overblown wants and desires while working to bring focus, purpose and direction into life.

The autumn experience of the human being is just that - working at bringing focus, purpose and direction into our own life after the more diffuse experience of summer. Our inner challenge is to recognize our responsibilities to ourselves and to the higher purposes for which we have been placed upon earth. This demands courage and the strength of will to see beyond the momentary and short-term gratifications to that which is ultimately more important for ourselves and world evolution.

At the same time as the final harvest is being gathered, so too is the harvesting of the outer forces of nature being concentrated within us, giving us the stuff whereby we can realize the potential to be truly human in the highest sense - recognizing our destiny and acting to fulfill it.

In many Waldorf schools throughout the world, the attempt is being made to bring life to the celebration of the Michaelmas festival; each school and its community seeking an appropriate form. Around September 29, the traditional date for Michaelmas, a pageant is presented which often includes a large dragon made by one class with others dressed as knights. Banners fly, music is made; then the teachers and older children are able to step up one by one and throw a spear at the dragon. A story is told of the victory of courage and clear intelligence over brute strength and/or crafty cleverness. Often there are stories of the slaying of dragons, and at other times the 'dragon' may take many different forms.

A few words about Halloween should be included. This, in its real meaning, has little to do with children, being a time of remembrance for departed souls. Because of commercialism, it has become something that we need to deal with as families. In my own family, costumes or masks were never bought for the children; rather, we always, as a family, talked about what we wanted to be - who we wanted to act out. Most often, characters from recently told stories, or later, personalities from legends, myths or history were favorites. Then we would make costumes from scratch with materials from our abundant 'costume box' of material and odd bits and scraps. In this way there was participation and excitement but not necessarily just the 'scary' kind. And we remembered the departed souls of historic or legendary figures. This enlarged the scope beyond the present personal to a sense of history, adventure, myth and legend. What better way than to reinforce learning through a fun filled experience!

When the children were young, we would have a party with
costumes, games and a story to which the children would
invite their friends. Later when the children were old
enough to go 'trick-or-treating,' we included Trick or
Treating for U.N.I.C.E.F. so that the activity would be
for more than just themselves. It was a gentle way of
expanding their consciousness by helping other children.
The 'haul' of goodies taken at Halloween would be kept
by the children, but we found that with guidance, it was
used responsibly and sometimes lasted as long as three
or four weeks, with just the one or two treats taken
each day.

and Winter Approaches

Aside from Thanksgiving, the next major festival and
perhaps the one that is most vivid for children is
the Christmas season. It is preceded by the four
weeks of Advent (which is counted by the four Sundays
before Christmas Day). The old European tradition of
Advent was that this time was spent in cleaning, baking,
decorating and inwardly preparing for the Christmas
event.

In my family, Advent usually began with a trip to the
nearby mountains sometime during the long Thanksgiving
week-end (American) to gather evergreen branches which
we could clip in the abundant forests while also
gathering moss from which we would make an Advent
garden. This foraging expedition took only several
hours, but it was a very special time of experiencing
and seeing the late autumn woods. There was the
excitement of looking near streams for moss and seeing
Mother Nature settled in for the winter. Wet feet,
scratched hands and a spirit of working together on this

98

little project made it one that we all looked forward to each year. As the children grew older, they knew exactly what we would need to bring, and the car would be packed very quickly with the saws and clippers for the branches and the trowel, shovel and plastic bags to gather and hold the moss. After two years it was a 'tradition' along with many others we had formed and when we did miss a year of doing this for one reason or another, we would all feel the loss and complain that we hadn't started Advent right.

Next came the making of an Advent wreath from some of the collected evergreens. Taking several wire hangers, we would refashion them into a circle approximately 18" - 24" in diameter, around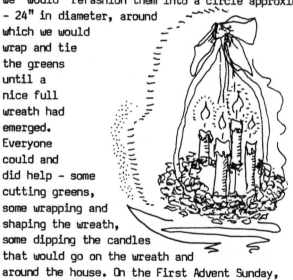
which we would
wrap and tie
the greens
until a
nice full
wreath had
emerged.
Everyone
could and
did help - some
cutting greens,
some wrapping and
shaping the wreath,
some dipping the candles
that would go on the wreath and
around the house. On the First Advent Sunday,
the wreath would be hung in a prominent place. The wreath looked quite grand with its four red candles and the four red ribbons that were joined together above to hold it in place.

A special space was chosen for the Advent garden. The area on which it was placed was carefully covered by sheets of plastic to protect against the moisture and stains that could result from the damp moss. With the help of stones, blocks of wood and boxes, we created a rough landscape over which the moss was laid to form a green carpet. This would become a wonderland miniature world, which represented the world of nature brought inside the home. In a sense it stands as a metaphor for the macrocosm and microcosm: the outer becoming the inner. The vast world becomes alive in our imagination and creativity. During the winter season, when we are thrown back into our inner world, we have the chance to become creators.

Over the years, we developed the tradition that each of the four Advent weeks had a special theme. The 'four' suggests itself to many things such as the directions, seasons, the four elements (earth, water, air, fire) and the four kingdoms of nature (mineral, plant, animal and the human being). Our favorite was to celebrate nature's four kingdoms.

On the First Advent Sunday, we would decorate the garden with each one's favorite rocks and crystals, and then light the first candle on the wreath in honor of the mineral kingdom. Each of us named our favorite rock or mineral and we sang several songs ("Deck the Halls" being an excellent one which speaks of the decorations and preparations for Christmas). Of course a story was told on that first Sunday which had something to do with the mineral kingdom.

Each succeeding Sunday, we added more to the garden. The second week; small plants, flowers, dried leaves or whatever imagination we had of the plant world. In the third week; favorite sea shells, toy animals, beeswax or clay animals represented the animal world. The last Sunday saw the appearance of the Creche with all the figures except the Christ child who would appear only on Christmas morning.

Each night during the week, just after dinner, is a good time to light the wreath with its one, two, three or four candles, depending on which week, and sing several songs. Each morning at breakfast, is a time to open that day's window on the Advent calendar. Advent calendars are sold in many stores; they have 'windows' that my be opened, one for each day of Advent. Some people make their own Advent calendars which are works of art and are used year after year. To make the dinner table different at this time, with a special cloth, some greens and a candle arrangement is good for it gives this time a sense of 'specialness.'

Over this four week period, the ritual itself becomes a rhythmic experience. The entire celebration of Advent (which means; the coming) can be kept quite simple or made ever more complex, but the important part to remember is to be consistent and not do it for a day or two and then again the following week for a few days. That is where children can be so disappointed and confused because they begin to doubt our sincerity, reliability and our devotion to what seems so important.

As children, we become devoted to the rituals in which we participate. This devotion becomes a nourishing factor in our lives, strengthening our will, creating the possibility of loyalty and devotion to later tasks. As adults, we cannot take this devotion lightly. Our need, as that of our children, is hopefully to be an intrinsic part of the ritual, instead of standing on the sideline being smug and/or removed from the process. The worst thing possible is that we don't take these things seriously.

Finally, Christmas draws near. For many years, until my oldest child was ten or twelve, the Christmas tree just appeared on our back deck or at the front door on the morning of December 24th. It would be the children who would discover it, shouting with glee that indeed we hadn't been forgotten. It mattered little that neighborhood tree lots abounded or that many of our neighbors had their trees earlier. Our tree was left by the Christmas tree fairy who selected and brought us one. It was as if we were blessed each year by mysterious forces that really did not need to be explained and couldn't be.

Christmas Eve day was spent in setting up the tree and decorating it. What joy as we poked through the 'Christmas Box' and rediscovered favorite decorations that had become old friends over many years!

The tree never had electric lights on it. Rather it had thirty-three candles - one for each year of the life of Jesus. Candle holders are still available in good candle shops and in over twenty years, there has never been a mishap. We found candles alight on the tree a most special and beautiful experience. In more northern areas, where the indoor heating quickly dries out the tree, candles may be dangerous and, after all, we do live in an electric age. But there is a wonderful feeling about candle light and even if candles are not on the tree there is plenty of good aesthetic reason to

102

have and light candles at this time of year. A few candles create a soft and beautiful environment that is far more soulful than blinking or bright lights.

Once again, how you do it in your home will be a matter of what feels right for you, but I have found that the building of anticipation is always very special. Christmas Eve should be a time of lighting the tree, singing carols and telling the Christmas story. It is a time of experiencing the "holy" part of the holiday; of coming into relationship with the mystery surrounding the birth of the child. It is the birth with its denial, pain and acceptance which needs to be celebrated and reenacted soulfully before there comes the onslaught of gifts. And anyhow, whose birthday are we celebrating? What gifts do we bring for the Christ Child or even for the spirit of the child? At least that is something we should think about in this season.

On Christmas morning, the children, even as teenagers, would find that their stockings, filled, had somehow moved from the mantle to their pillows. They knew that they were to stay in their rooms until the tree had once again been lighted. Then we would go room to room in a solemn procession singing a carol which would bring us, still in our robes, to the tree where all the presents we had placed under the tree the night before had been joined by others.

Perhaps a further word about the opening of gifts is worthwhile. Even though it may take a much longer time it would seem that each and every gift should be opened separately with everyone paying attention to what will emerge from the wonderful womb of the gift wrapping. Opening a gift is like a birth or the emergence into the world of someone's creativity. It deserves to be noticed and appreciated. In all too many homes everyone grabs for their gifts and each person opens their own as quickly as possible. Wrappings and ribbons fly, cards get lost and in the end it is only the gift (whose creative giver may already be forgotten) which stands there like an orphan. If we do give gifts at Christmas, the least we can do is to give and receive them with dignity, grace and with ritual.

Perhaps this gives enough of an idea of celebrating festivals. Again the reminder that each family needs to find its own way, but by all means build traditions that are special and right for your circumstances. Some will begin because you have thought them out carefully while others will begin casually or accidently and then seem so special and right. Whatever you do, let it have a certain style and majesty, that will help to build the strength of fabric for your family's uniqueness.

Birthdays

Birthdays are a unique form of celebration because each of us has our own day. This day makes the beginning of our own year. It is our starting point, our point of entry into physical existence and it deserves to be celebrated as a remembrance of our start in life. Here is where gifts and presents are most appropriate, for don't we need special things when we begin a long, exciting journey? As the cycle of the year comes around once more we begin the next stage of our ongoing journey through life.

From a cosmological view our birthday signifies one revolution of the earth around the sun and an approximate return to how the stars were at the time of our birth. The heavenly configuration of planets and stars will never be quite the same, so we are in the paradoxical situation of returning to our origins only to find that we always find something new. While we look back we will find, even in space, that the situation is continually evolving, changing and shifting. I find this to be a powerful metaphor for our journey through life and that while we may retain an image of how it was at our birth we will never find exactly those conditions, astronomically, again in our lifetime.

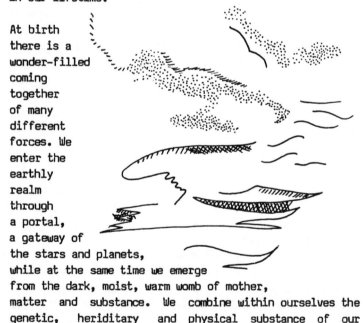

At birth there is a wonder-filled coming together of many different forces. We enter the earthly realm through a portal, a gateway of the stars and planets, while at the same time we emerge from the dark, moist, warm womb of mother, matter and substance. We combine within ourselves the genetic, heriditary and physical substance of our parents and have our own uniqueness and our own history.

Rudolf Steiner gave us an image, in the form of a meditation which allows us the possibility of coming to an understanding of the essential nature of the human being:

My Head bears the being of the resting stars.
My Breast harbours the life of the wandering Stars[Planets].
My Body lives and moves amid the Elements.
This am I.[13]

Often, in Waldorf Schools the birthday celebration, especially in preschool, kindergarten and the primary grades takes on the wonderful image of the child being the prince or princess for the day, wearing a golden crown and a lovely, royal looking cape. On this day there are special privileges such as being first to do various activities or even leading them. There is a regal quality about the day and at these young ages, while children are less self-conscious, the enactment of the image, done with ritual, becomes a special and moving experience.

Needless to say, the presents given at a birthday should be thoughtful. One idea that may guide us is: What does my child need on the journey for the coming year? What will best help in my child's inner and outer development? This does not mean that the gift will be one that is so serious that it will not be enjoyed. Our challenge as parents is to help our children to grow and develop. When we go shopping, having that in mind may guide us to something that has a deeper and more lasting quality rather than only being caught by the latest fad or commercial venture that is really of little value to the child except that it is cute or tickles our sense of humour.

As children grow older and celebrate their eighth or ninth birthday something new can be added to the birthday celebration aside from the cake, presents and party. Set aside a time for an intimate sharing of the close (or expanded) family where the birthday person (and this includes each of the adults on their birthday) can say a few words about the past year; some high  points, low points, challenges, successes and failures and what the year has meant. This should be followed with an expression of what this coming year may bring. In this way a sense of time and a feeling for the ebb and flow of life gradually begins to be built. How many of us actually do take stock of our lives at this significant moment each year? If we did we might begin to see the patterns of our own lives; the rhythms, and motions. Perhaps we might gain some meaning in the countless separate events that make up our long and often challenging adventure through the forest of life. When we begin to put the individual pieces of life's puzzle together, a picture slowly emerges. The pieces gradually form parts of the picture and the parts interrelate until in old age we finally may grasp a sense of wholeness about our lives.

This certainly is not an easy task but we should give to our children a feeling that there is hardly anything more important than their gaining a meaning in the story of their lives. Without at least working on grasping our story or myth (for it is actually more than simply a factual recitation - in fact it is larger than life, as are the great myths of the world) how can we ever hope to grasp the story and meaning of what goes on in the world around us.

The most precious of all the birthday presents we can give to our children, loved ones and ourselves, is this moment to focus on the events and experiences of our everyday lives and to begin to weave the myth of our life story. We can look at each birthday as a rite of passage and be there with our full feeling of warmth, love, support and consciousness. An integral part of this gathering should happen after our children have had their say. Then we as parents may also say something, acting as a mirror to reflect what we have seen during the preceeding year and what we hope will happen in the future. Being honest is important as long as we are also supportive, positive and constructive.

Presents

As we all know, but find hard to practice, it isn't how many or how expensive the presents are, that is really important, but how meaningful they are. While it is very difficult to be consistent, it is very important to make as many presents as possible and to encourage children to do the same. That becomes a wonderful way of giving of yourself that has far more meaning than spending money on something lavish. My experience has been from doll house, to wooden trucks and wagons, stuffed dolls and animals, hand sewn clothes, pictures, cards or candles. My children have knitted various things such as scarves and hats and have often given craft projects that they made in school, or beautiful paintings or drawings done in class.

I have, when buying , aimed at good quality wooden toys, fine books, beautiful shells and rocks and have generally tried to avoid plastic, shoddy and unaesthetic things.

A gift says something about the giver and where possible it should be representative of your thoughts and feelings about the person who is to receive it. As adults and guides to our children, to bestow a gift should also have the function of teaching. We give a physical gift but it should also nourish the soul of the child. If there is no inner nourishment from the gift it will be like stones instead of bread.

In today's 'hard sell' world of merchandising, many children are being brainwashed to want particular products that are not necessarily best for them and we as parents must take on the responsibility - out of love for our children - to say no when we feel a particular toy or product (that the child is crying for) becomes an issue. This isn't always easy as we can be made to feel guilty of depriving our child. Yet, we must look at it another way and realize that many products are put on the store shelves and in display cases with no moral, aesthetic or educational consciousness. It is therefore our right and duty to protect our children from something that is not good for them - even it is means a momentary confrontation.

In the long run, our children will love us the more and certainly have respect for us because we have been true and consistent to our own standards and ideals. This builds the respect, confidence and trust in a relationship that is meant for a lifetime. The momentary disappointment in the child must be weighed against the inner frustrations of shoddy and inappropriate toys that are bought to appease misguided, miseducated and commercial tastes.

Yet the question needs to be asked: Would you feed your child something that would not be good - or worse yet - may not be healthy for the body? Toys and things that surround the child are, at least potential nourishment for the soul life. Are we to give empty calories of soul food? Are we to surround our children with things and create an environment that is not nourishing? Worse yet, are we to stifle the inner growth of the thinking, feeling and willing capacity of our child?

Living in Space

The Environment

The space or environment in which we live is very important to us - or at least it should be. It says something about who we are; our image of ourselves and who and what we may want to be. In the animal world, birds create nests and beavers work diligently to build their dams and homes. Bees, wasps and ants work as communities to fashion rather elaborate homes that are quite complex. None of the above assert their individualities in their home building. What they produce comes out of deep seated instinct and varies little from beaver dam to beaver dam or from hive to hive. In a sense their homes are perfect as representations of their species rather than as individual creative endeavors.

But for human beings, since earliest times (and even today with so called "primitive" or traditional peoples) there is usually the urge to somehow individualize the family space. It may be done in any number of ways, but almost always, we can see that each home, tent, yurt, hut or igloo has had some aspect, some stamp that this

111

family or person is different from the rest of the tribe, group and community.

One of our greatest tasks as human beings upon the earth, is to individualize. If we trace the history of civilization with an eye focused on the development of consciousness we can not help but be struck at the great paradox of original unity flowing toward diversity in such areas as language, custom, dress, housing while at the same time the world has grown steadily smaller, closer and more easily accessible. From very few original root languages we have formed our Tower of Babel of diverse tongues which now in the contemporary world can be seen and heard instantaneously anywhere in the world.

All of this can be tied to the struggle to gradually individualize. Rudolf Steiner spoke of this present age as the Consciousness Soul epoch; a time when the last vestiges of tribal blood and even family ties need to be broken away from the old unconscious ways. Now we need to have ties and bonds that emerge out of freedom and conscious choice.

The cause of so much pain, struggle and unhappiness is that we are not conscious that this is, in fact, our task on earth - to become fully individualized so that in conscious, responsible freedom we may serve the creative spirits, the earth, our fellow travellers on earth and our self.

We have lost the instinct of the animals and their relatively perfect relationship with the environment. In exchange we have the possibility of freedom, of choice and of consciousness. We have left Paradise and we must make our way in what sometimes appears to be a God-forsaken world. And the world of matter presents to us a way of expression, an actual, physical resistance, a canvas upon which we can express our selves and a place in which we can be.

If a 'man's home is his castle' it is also one major way of self-expression. This demands an awareness that although we may not be able to determine much of our environment, we can at least determine where and how we use that which is closest to us in our dress and in our home.

Money, or lack of it, is no excuse for not being able to create what you are. I have seen the most beautiful homes furnished very simply and artistically on a 'shoe string.' I have seen some of the poorest people dressed in clean, neat and beautiful clothes that expressed the owner's individuality. It isn't price nor number of things that ultimately matters. Rather it is care, taste and consciousness that go into making the selections and setting the style of your own expression. Whether it is carefully selected form garage sales, second hand shops or the best boutique in town - what we select is our free choice and says to the world something about ourselves.

For myself and my children I have tried to keep this in mind, realizing that what we do also has a profound effect on our children's aesthetic taste. Whether we are neat and clean, orderly and organized and use discrimination and taste in dress and in our own space gives a non-verbal but strong message to our children.

Woe the parent who shouts at children to clean up the toys and yet leaves the study or kitchen a perpetual mess! That breeds a message of insincerity and cynicism that can and does go very deep.

We don't necessarily want, nor in a practical sense will we ever have, our children end up with tastes identical to our own. The point is, that our standard of care, concern and love for the environment is something that we take seriously enough to deal with consistently and lovingly.

The strange paradox that I have found is that many of the most ardent materialists are actually people who have little understanding, concern or care for their environment; they can always buy another thing and replace it when it breaks. The disregard for physical things can lead to an unhealthy relationship to and lack of reverence for the effort of other people in the world to make available the goods and services we want, need and use. It is, ultimately, a spiritual matter; how we use the material world and if we realize that the physical world is a manifestation of spiritual forces then we must take the course of using the 'things' of the world with reverence and respect. It may seem obvious to say it, but every single thing we use has its starting point in nature. The human being doesn't create material. Our act of creativity is in the transformation of matter from one state to another. It is quite a wonderful thought, that is awe-inspiring, to realize

that when we turn on an electric light
we are experiencing the light of the sun
that has been stored in coal or oil for eons
and has been released through a complex form of
ingenious processes culminating in the electricity
we take for granted.

Dealing with matter is one of the highest forms of human
experience. We become like the gods in that we are able
to create and transform that which is around us. It is
only human beings, of all the creatures of the earth,
who are able and seem to need to so drastically alter
the bounties of nature. Whether it be food, clothing or
shelter, we use only a minimal amount of material
directly as nature gives it to us. So we are beings
needing to create and use nature's offerings. We have
the freedom to use nature responsibly and aesthetically,
or to literally rape and violate the earth.

This issue of the consciousness with which we approach
the material we use is one fraught with deeply moral,
ethical and religious questions.

Perhaps one of the greatest tragedies of today is that,
rather than approaching nature in a gesture of reverence
and gratitude, we attack her with a rapacious, greedy
and thoughtless attitude. It is hardly necessary to
recount all the ills and crises that people have caused
to Earth; the literature is more than abundant. What we
each have to do in addition to conserving and recycling
is to develop the attitude whereby we become even more
conscious of how we use material; how we approach it and
how we increase the beauty of the world around us so
that our souls may be healed while we also heal the
earth.

Our environment does actually have an effect on how we feel and who we are. Many of us will go into the woods or the mountains for a weekend and feel better for having been there. Yet we will not recognize that the ugly office, shop, plant in which we work actually decreases our energy level, making us depressed and/or angry and irritable.

The issue may be color, the fabrics we wear, the noise level or light intensity, temperature or the general aesthetic ambiance. All of these may affect us as vitally (although more subtly) than the food we eat. The human being has become less sensitive and less conscious of bodily conditions as well as soul conditions. For many, it seems a virtue to 'tough it out.' That may be necessary at times and yet we have paid a high price to buy into the hardening process.

While we may not easily be able to change the space around us; where we work, shop, or play we can at least look to our home and ourselves as very important starting points.

Have you ever felt the difference between wearing an all cotton shirt and one made of polyester? The cotton breathes, allowing air to circulate; whereas, the polyester confines and holds in the body heat; not allowing for a free exchange of the body with its environment.
We all need to redevelop a sensitivity to the fabrics and materials that we use. That is not to say that we should never use any synthetic materials; for obviously they have their place and are marvelous developments of technology. My experience is that using natural materials such as cotton, wool, and silk, give to the

atmosphere around us a resilience that synthetics just do not have.

It is especially important for young children to be surrounded by natural materials as the infant is so much more sensitive than the adult. It is frustrating to shop for baby clothes, toys, bedding and so on, and find the market flooded with abundant and relatively cheap (in comparison to natural materials) synthetics. It takes the extra effort to find cotton and wool for the young child - but in the long run, it is well worth the effort and does begin to create in our own will, the consciousness that what we have around and for our children will be the best that we can get.

This whole approach - to be conscious of the materials we use for ourselves and our children - is in fact, a question of consciousness and sensitivity. It is also one of having the will to persevere until we find what is right for us and what, in the long run, will give us pride and pleasure because of the care that has been taken in the selection.

Art, Literature and Music

Our home environment includes the things with which we are surrounded; clothing, furniture, plants, and also the activities and interests which we do in that space. The things we do, the interests and attitudes we have when we do them are also a reflection of who we are and what we are striving to become. It is just as true to say that it isn't enough to have a beautiful home if nothing much is happening within it, as it is to point to an unbeautiful home as a reflection of soul cut off from matter.

117

A healthy home has a variety of activities and interests going on in it. If we as adults have our own interests, hobbies and activities we will be all the more interesting to ourselves and those around us. It sets an example for our children; they can see that the world is full of interesting things to do both inside and outside the home.

We need to fill our home, and most of all, ourselves, with good art, literature and music not only as consumers but as participants. One of the seductive traps of today's world is that there is so much available in the market place of beautiful, professionally produced 'art' that many people feel that they themselves can't compete with what is available. Further, that the results of their own creative labors aren't nearly good enough - so why bother? To that, I would say that a song sung lovingly by a mother or father is far preferable to the most exquisite recording, because in the act of learning the song and sharing it, you create a bond that is uniquely woven by your effort and your caring. You have given yourself in a truly intimate way, and that is what one aspect of artistic expression is really all about - the giving of oneself. When we can learn to do that, even in as imperfect a way as we may feel we do, we have touched transcendent qualities within ourselves that are very special.

A small practical detail: children's pictures put into a nice frame often look more lovely than when they are stuck onto the door of the fridge with wrinkled and tattered corners. It gives children joy, or for that matter, anyone, to see their picture nicely framed and hung in a prominent place. I would hope that every

member of the family has at least one frame for their
latest or best work.

That is not to say that we shouldn't appreciate the
artistic endeavors of others or that we have to do
everything ourselves; there must be a blend of creating
and consuming. Once we have begun to create for
ourselves, we are all the more sensitive to the efforts
and abilities of others; thus, we can become far more
appreciative of what goes into the creative process in
general.

A family, as mentioned earlier, needs to have a variety
of interests and activities. It is up to us as adults to
bring that range of activity into the home. Here, there
is also the question of finding the appropriate
activities, not only for ourselves, but for the various
ages and stages of childhood. One of the most important
rights of children is that they be treated as children
in a way that understands and is sensitive to their
stage of development. In our sharing and doing as a
family, there are the moments when we need to choose
what might be our own need and blend it with the needs
of our mate and our children.

For instance, if we enjoy listening to music of a
particular type our need to listen may have to be
moderated by the children who are around. Their inner
need may be to have quiet or to have a blend of
experiences rather than only the one type of music which
we have come to appreciate.

Particularly with music, the constant sound as a
background while other things are being done or
conversations are being held, creates a split

119

concentration which is basically unhealthy. We ought to be able to give ourselves over fully to the activity in which we are engaged. Much of the sound we have on in the background tends to be part of our addiction to activity and our fear of aloneness. Having silence in the environment can be a frightening experience for some people now-a-days, as we have become so used to background noise of one sort or another. It has become a societal addiction and it takes an act of will to break the habit. Try it, if you are 'addicted' and feel what can happen in a constructive silence. The potential for hearing your own 'still small voice' within becomes more possible when the outside noises are stilled and you have begun to work through the upset to your system and the fear it engenders when that silence becomes a tangible factor. This is especially important for the baby and young child, but it is vital for all of us.

Many infants and small children are addicted to background noise from a very early age. They have hardly started life when they are confronted with radios being played in hospital nurseries, in cars and at home. No wonder that when all the noise stops the baby is jolted into another, frightening state. If normally it has been noisy, the silence becomes threatening.

Hardly a moment goes by in the modern world when there is not some background noise. How difficult it is to find relative quiet for even a few minutes. The constant buzz seems comforting for most people because they are so accustomed to it and this seems to have something to do with the reassuring feeling that we are not alone. That is such a strong urge in some people that when alone at home many people will have radios and television sets going in various rooms. When our children experience this incessant background noise there is a gradual desensitizing of the hearing and a message that to be without the constant buzz is not an acceptable way to be in the world. How to listen to our own sounds or how to make our own sounds are discounted questions when you have readily available sounds of all sorts right there, instantaneously.

The insidious invasion of sound in our lives has further been intensified by the "Walkman Revolution" which has expanded the frontiers into our ears and out onto our bicycles, on our walks and jogs, onto buses and even in bed. Many children are now so addicted to these portable tape players/radios that they literally cannot go to sleep without having the earphones operational as their heads touch the pillow.

I had a recent experience of riding in a car with a family where each person (Mother, Father and two children ages 11 and 13) had a cassette and earphones so that they would be free to hear what they each wanted. There was peace and quiet for me but no communication amongst the family and while there was no fighting about who was to listen to what there was also no give and take, no compromise, no expanding of horizons. Each person could follow their individual path, alone and without the social challenge that helps make us caring people. For me it was a chilling image: Each person mildly sedated, left to their own world like the old picture of the opium den where each person was left to meet their own reveries in their withdrawal from the world.

Television

Television, along with videos, radios, stereos, tape decks and the numerous variations, is something like the story of the Trojan horse. After ten years of frontal assault and heroic battles, the Greeks could not defeat the city of Troy, where walls remained standing. The Greeks realized another strategy was necessary and built the Great Wooden Horse which they left outside the gates. The Greek armies withdrew from the plain of battle and the Greek ships sailed away. The Trojans rejoiced and opened their gates, brought the beautiful horse inside the walls and celebrated their survival. As they slept off the celebrations, the Greeks, hidden within the horse emerged and opened the gates to the Greek armies who had silently crept back to Troy.

Beware of Greeks bearing gifts! These wonderful electronic additions to the household; these signs and symbols of affluence and technological mastery are having the effect of eroding the heart out of the family. The heart which circulates and communicates with all parts of the whole; which brings nourishment and takes away waste; which refreshes and brings together the various parts; which makes a living whole, an entity, out of the surging individual cells. This heart is being eroded, isolated and mechanized. It is losing its organic rhythm and being forced to march to a different beat.

If the family in the car can go its separate ways (inwardly) as they hurtle down the road, how difficult it will be to build the feeling for the whole when the parts are being overvalued and emphasized.

All the electronic media have the same basic effect on the family which is to divert attention and energy from human, personal interaction and relationship. Simply put, it becomes very difficult to relate, intimately, when the stereo or the radio is going, and it gets close to impossible when the television is playing. The combined audio and visual impact tends to overwhelm conversation. Eyes and ears are both being beckoned and the rapid delivery and catchy rhythm around television programming further grips us so that conversation gradually halts and attention is focused on the set. What conversation that may continue is sporadic and elementary. Reflection, careful phrasing and thoughtful speaking and/or listening are difficult because of the time restraints and the split attention.

The literature on the effects of television on the home and more specifically on children is vast and controversial. All too often the television debate is focused on the quality of programming and most certainly the quality needs vast improvement. More important is the whole question of whether the activity of watching television (no matter what the quality of programming) is beneficial for young children. Particularly, for children before their eighth or ninth birthday, television viewing is a harmful activity. The argument is quite simple: when children are watching television they are not playing, reading, talking, creating or being active. These are all intrinsically important to the process of growth and development physically, emotionally, psychologically and intellectually. Body, soul and spirit are cheated by children passively sitting in front of television sets. The little factual knowledge which might be obtained by viewing some better programs is offset by the violence, commercialism triteness and absurdity of most programming. But that argument may be set aside as we ask: What are children not doing while they watch television? They are missing the live, living experience of exploring the world, of playing, creating and struggling with other human beings and with the world of matter.

Children are taught a major lesson when watching television; that they can passively observe the world and receive stimulation, entertainment, knowledge by sitting back: "I don't have to do anything. I don't have to take risks. I don't have to engage with people nor do I have to "get my hands dirty" in this world. All I need to do is flip the switch and it will all come to me. Not only that, but I can tune the world on and off at will."

A false, jaded and cynical picture of the world is soon formed by those who are more extreme television watchers. They are, in fact, addicts; hooked on the fix of stimulation they get from watching their shows.

On an adult level I encounter many people who derive most of their ideas from talk shows which are carefully stage managed to give simplistic ideas in convincing ways through guests who are full of energy, charm and vitality which the average viewer doesn't have and envies. Too many conversations center around what was heard and seen on television rather than what was thought about or experienced in real life.

Children get the idea, through their own experience of television, and through seeing adults, that what goes on in the set may be more important than what happens in life.

One other aspect of television: As teachers we see ever more activity arising out of television characters, cartoons and various programs. There are times when children seem consumed by particular figures who they have no choice but to act and play out. Often this leads to violent and generally aggressive play. Here again these children are deprived of large areas of choice in which their imaginations may be activated. Because imitation is such a strong part of the younger children's way of learning the world, the strong images seen in movies and television will tend to block out more subtle images that may come through stories or out of their own inner life. Educators see great difficulty in children's play; it is no longer free and creative and is bound to rigid patterns taken from media characters. Imagination suffers for there is less allowable range in play. Sophisticated toys which are cleverly marketed along with many movies and television programs are "needed" to complete the pictures to be "played" out. No longer is a stick or a block transformable into an infinite number of things. Rare are the children who can unselfconsciously be dragons, witches, knights, cowboys, princesses or whatever they inwardly need or want to be. All too often we can observe that children's play is driven by the outside force of the media.

The role of television in the home is to attack activity, imagination and creativity, tending to encourage passivity. It is a form of narcotic and should be treated as such. Children who are addicted to television go through the same symptoms as other kinds of addicts. The television often becomes a dominant force in the household around which arises many rituals, customs and conflicts, which may affect all the members of the house.

In many cases I have suggested to families that they go "cold turkey" by pulling the plug and abandoning all television watching in the home. This is painful, dramatic and very effective. For several days or a week or two there are tears, tantrums, nervousness and feelings of alienation. The withdrawal period is tense and needs support, warmth, compassion and love. After a week or so family members begin to rediscover alternative activities during these periods when the television had previously dominated the home. Games are played, painting, drawing and reading, story telling and conversations begin to be practiced; activities that previously had been lost or forgotten. In a few weeks families will find that given the television, people are too busy to take up their time with it. Of course this drastic approach doesn't work unless there is commitment from the parents who may have to also recognize their addiction.

For most homes with television the solution may not necessarily be so drastic. The best approach seems to be to recognize television as a part of our society and to use this potentially addictive narcotic in a healthy way. How wonderful it is for children to see an example of moderation, sensitivity, common sense and control of self in a difficult situation. As role models we need to be serious about being as conscious as possible in each situation.

Television should be a part of each household and children after the age of six or seven should be exposed to it in a very moderate degree. I found that choosing one program a week which the whole family watched together and talked about and shared was sufficient until near adolescence where perhaps another program

126

or two were gradually added. In this way the children, while not having full and unrestricted access did feel they had a family who lived in the big world and shared some important values with everybody (children need to feel that they belong to society) while there were also family values that were important and good.

The extreme of absolutely no television usually drives children to friends or relatives where they take massive overdoses to make up for their felt deprivation and then feel guilt for going counter to the family value system.

How we as a family handle the issue of television becomes a very important indicator of how we will deal with other difficult issues of potential addiction and the upholding of the family value system. The extremes of a) watch as much as you like, or b) absolutely no watching, create a) addictive personalities or b) potential alienation from family values and perhaps guilt for being untrue or estranged from the culture in which they live. This may build to other resentments in adolescence.

This is a delicate area and takes consciousness, humour and sensitivity so that children may be protected from a harmful experience. With enough skill we can keep children on our side.

Literature

The literature to which we expose our children is a very important concern. The stories we tell from the beginning, the books we read to them and later the books that they read leave deep, lasting images and memories which help to form the mood of their own inner life. Even as adults, a book that we read may give us images that we carry for days and weeks. A vivid scene may flash up in us and we will relive its power or poignancy and this may affect our mood of soul in a profound way. With young children this can happen even more deeply.

We must be very sensitive to the images which we present to children, particularly asking the questions of ourselves: is it appropriate to the age of the child? Is it something that will help the child to grow? Is it something that is truly moral from a higher, wider and deeper point of view? Is it a true image, or is it one that is cute or clever from an adult point of view?

Much of children's literature is entertaining to adults; for they are the ones who usually select and pay for it, but if we have developed sufficient sensitivity for our children we would find that the images often presented in children's books are silly, untrue and in fact, not conducive to the inner growth of the child. How do we determine this? Can we even be judges of literature as well as everything else we need to do in life? Obviously, the answer needs to be yes and we have to develop not only the sensitivity to the images presented in children's literature but also to have the courage to take responsibility for making the appropriate choices. The time will come soon enough when your children will be making their own choices - but while you can, and even later where you have some input, you need to make the choices that represent the highest aspects of the human being - rather than the banal.

As we well know, the minds of young children are very alive, imaginative and open; their sense of the world is quite different than the adult's. It is not bound to logical, sequential, rational thinking and is free to live in what we as adults only touch upon in our dreams, or in moments of artistic creativity. Here time, and space and the logical order of our day-waking consciousness gives way to a far more fluid and flexible flow of events and experiences in our dream world.

Even further, children being closer to their origins in the spiritual world have perceptions and inner experiences which connect them differently to the physical world. While the adult may speak of dwarves, fairies, and other elemental beings with a certain whimsy, children, in fact, experience this as truth. While the adult may tell about a talking bear or wolf; the children know that animals do talk to each other. It is only later in childhood that this knowing, intuitive experience of the world fades, usually around the ninth year.

When we tell a 'story,' children, having faith in us as a true guide for them upon the earth, accept it as truth. Thus, the stories we tell should be true - ones that we ourselves can believe. That is not to say that they need be logical, rational or scientifically verifiable - not at all. They need be true from the point of view of the 'child' within us. They need to 'ring' true with real imaginations of the physical, spiritual, inner and outer worlds rather than be clever flights into the fantastic. There is a far cry between 'Green Eggs and Ham' and 'Hansel and Gretel.' We need to sense that the story has its starting point in true archetypes and gestures of the world. It needs to represent, in a living way, the kingdoms of nature; the elements of earth, water, air and fire; the basic elements of the human being and the spiritual forces that lie behind the sense perceptual world.

The old fairy tales generally do this in a most wonderful way. If we 'live' into the various stories we find, if we are open and receptive, then they speak to our striving life of soul. Many folk tales do the same; as well as the great myths and legends of the world. The vast resource at our disposal, if we were to choose only the great stories of the past, would be enough for several lifetimes of enjoyment. They represent, as Jung would say, the collective memory of the human race. Is there a better way to grow into the world than by connecting with the experiences and expressions of our ancestors in all cultures of the past? As children still retain the openness to the greater truths of the world out of which they have come and into which they have entered, the language of this great body of literature speaks directly to their inner being. Of course, there is much of modern children's literature that is excellent, true and aesthetic. Any trip to a good bookstore will produce many fine examples of children's stories.

The big challenge is to have the discernment to choose the right book or story for your child appropriate to the age and stage of development in that particular moment. In fact, most of the wonderful folk, fairy tales, legends and myths are not appropriate for very young children - especially before age five. Here we must be quite selective as the stories of greater complexity need to be held off until later.

The most appropriate stories for younger children, as mentioned earlier, are simple nature stories and very simple stories that are light in their mood and have much repetition.

Young children love to look at picture books and have stories read to them. We need to have the right supply on hand. It is probably more important to have artistic and fine quality books early on than at any time. The cheap, mass produced books found in the local supermarket are generally of the 'cute' variety, Very few of them either have good story content or truly artistic illustrations. Although they often start from an old Grimm's fairy tale, they have been so changed that the original meaning and significance of the story has been drastically watered down or even altered. The pictures are often more like caricatures or cartoons. We

131

must look at these books with and through the eyes of our children and then ask ourselves whether that is really what we want them to see as presentations of the world. The young child is open and trusting and we have to take the responsibility not to betray that trust.

Look for books that have artistic layouts where the colors are subtle and the figures are not caricatures. Try to avoid hard outlines around the figures and garish colors. Read the content and distinguish between things that are fantastic and those that have true imaginations.

Distinguishing between fantasy and imagination is not an easy or clean cut matter. In fact, the two words are often used interchangeably. For our purpose I would suggest that fantasy arises out of the personal unconscious, influenced by our own experience, tastes and thought processes. Imagination arises out of the individual's perception, of what Jung would call, the collective unconscious and Steiner would speak of as the world of the etheric formative forces. This is the unseen world that is larger than us, out of which come the archetypal patterns which lie behind what we see and experience in the world. The imaginal world is the world of images that are "larger than life" and "more real than real." This is the stuff of legends, myths and the great religious writings; images and pictures that speak universally to the hearts and minds of most people and have done so through the ages. Truly imaginative people may perceive an archetype and put it in a modern form which will still retain a sense of universality.

Whereas fantasies may be cute and attractive at some level they usually lack the connection with the archetypal world; the place of formative patterns and universal truths. One can sense an "invented" quality rather than something which has organically grown out of roots firmly fixed in the depths of the unconscious and heights of the world of spirit.

The sharing and discovery of good literature is a life long pursuit for many of us. It is a way of connecting with the world and nourishing the soul. The reading of books and the telling of stories should not end when the children enter school or when they begin to read for and by themselves.

In my family we continued that sharing right through the teenage years where we told each other about good books that we were reading or had just completed. We shared passages that had particular beauty, power or meaning to us and we actually continued on occasion to read aloud favorite books, stories or articles. That was a wonderful sharing.

I have found in my family experiences and in many families I know, that children become avid readers not by telling or urging them to do so, but because the excitement of great literature gets 'into the blood' and is part of their nourishment from early on. Little has to be said about reading a book when children have been brought up hearing great stories. It becomes the next logical step for them to pick up books and read as it is already a natural part of their life's activities.

I know of one single parent, a mother, who has two sons who made it an absolutely sacrosanct ritual to read to her sons every evening. As time went on they would take

turns reading to each other and selecting what the family would share. Even into their late teenage years, they shared this group ritual of exciting experiences that helped open to them the world of literature, history, mythology, geography, drama and just sheer enjoyment.

Whether it be music, literature, the visual arts or anything else that is of interest to you, as adult people, it becomes a matter of finding the appropriate ways of sharing with the whole family in an aesthetic, interesting and living way. Even though our children will, at some point, disagree with our choices and our taste and may well need to experiment with the latest 'pop' or teen culture, if we have provided good, rich, profound and aesthetic experiences they will have a foundation upon which to build a richly satisfying 'inner' world when they become adults.

As inhabitants of the earth, we live in the rhythms of time and in the environment of space. As creative human beings we have the potential to go beyond that which has been given to us and to actually enhance, enrich and enliven this world. Each minute can be made an 'eternal' experience and where we tread can become a 'heavenly garden.' What we do to mold our space is up to us as a richly creative enterprise. In fact, for many people who do not consider themselves 'artistic,' the molding and creating of their own environment and the style in which they live, may in fact be their artistic achievement.

134

Dynamics of the Family

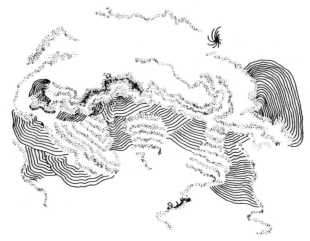

Once again there has been the blend of time and space;
that is, the <u>quality</u> of time spent in an environment
made rich with important, meaningful experiences. The
points to be emphasized are ones which I hope recur
throughout this book: quality transcends quantity,
spirit gives meaning to matter. Without consciousness,
the things we say, do or have, possess little meaning.
The deep inner sense for the aesthetic, when it
underlies our lives, makes more out of what we have; it
breathes life, light and meaning into them. Part of the
aesthetic is the sense for what is appropriate, i.e. the
right approach at the right time or the right thing in
the right place.

The converse is so often the case. People will often do the 'right thing' at the wrong time or place a beautiful object in a 'wrong setting.' The beauty of a 'weed' is seldom appreciated by the gardener who pulls it out of the carefully prepared garden.

The context and relationship surrounding a word, deed or object can be as important as the 'thing' in itself. Just as wine, candlelight and soft music may be inappropriate for a hard driving business meeting so too will nursery rhymes and fairy tales not be right for most teenagers who are trying to express themselves in the context of the age in which they live.

As parents we need, on the one hand, to keep our own standards which may have a timelessness of their own, while, on the other hand, recognizing the changing and evolving needs of the growing family. This delicate balance must have its starting point in the home for here is the creation of adults who have tastes, opinions and creativity and whose expression of themselves is an important act in their own lives. There also needs to be sensitivity for what may be needed by their children at each stage of their lives. Our inner responsibility (i.e. what we owe to ourselves) is to be striving for a deeper understanding of ourselves. As we are on that path of being vulnerable, open, questioning and working we may have the insights as to who we are, ourselves, and perhaps who those around us are or who they are striving to be.

The question raised earlier in the book: that as parents
we need to consider ourselves as people first, needs
once again to be raised. We have seen
that in the context of time
and space we must deal
with who we are in
order to establish
a truly comfortable
family rhythm or
a home environment
that says
something
about
'me.'

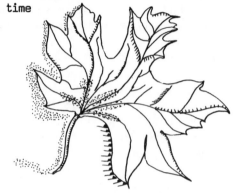

Perhaps one brief example will suffice to illustrate
what is now meant here: Robert enjoys staying up until
midnight on most nights and yet is quite able to awaken
at 7:00 a.m. in order to go to work. Jane on the other
hand feels exhausted by 10:00 p.m. most nights, and
needs to be asleep by that hour if she is to function
efficiently and creatively the next day. For them as
people and as partners in life, that discrepancy in
rhythms and in bodily and psychic needs will have to be
worked out for Robert and Jane to relate smoothly.

This difference in rhythm may affect how the evening is
structured; their bedtime rituals and activities, and so
on. In a relationship where each can express his/her own
needs, capabilities, feelings and ideas some creative
solution will evolve that will recognize the needs of
each. Accommodation will have to be made which respects
each partner so that each feels comfortable with the
solution. The wonderful thing is that for each couple
confronted with this particular (seemingly minor)

difference, who are able to work it through with a reasonable degree of consciousness, each will arrive at their own unique answer or solution. Even more interesting and exciting, is the prospect that with time, Robert and Jane's solution will evolve, change, and readjust to meet new and different needs that one or both may have.

So, we are not only 'Robert's wife' or 'Jane's husband.' We are single individuals with particular and unique needs which must be blended with others within the family unit in order to have some degree of success in the relationship. The more self-conscious, self-aware and centered we are, the more we are able to share, give and be sensitive to the other. To be selfish has the element of insecurity, of needing to protect one's self, of not knowing one's self well enough so that the physical and emotional demands on our static view of our self becomes a major threat.

Being able to process one's needs, fears, desires and aspirations with another makes it possible for a relationship to grow as the individuals within the

relationship are growing. It takes great courage at
times to admit inadequacy, fear and ignorance even as it
takes courage to say 'I love you' when you are not sure
what the response may be. There is a great risk in being
vulnerable in front of another person and all too often
in a love relationship, we (especially men) want to hide
our weakness because of fear that we might not be loved
as much if our strengths aren't seen to be shining
and unblemished. Yet it is precisely this very
vulnerability, this ability to admit
that we have weaknesses and
the process of sharing
them, that in the
long run allows
for love and
mutual respect
to be deepened,
to take
root and
to grow more
expansively.

Trust and confidence are basic
ingredients that must be present
if there is to be any real and deep
sharing. First, there is the trust and
confidence in oneself to be strong enough
to be exposed. Enough self-affirmation and
self-love (i.e. that I am a worthy person in my
own eyes as well as in the eyes of others) so that
confrontation, criticism and disagreement will not be
absolutely devastating. Then, there is the trust and
confidence in the other. This comes with time,
experience and willingness to really work through the
rough edges as well as to enjoy the smooth times.

All the above also applies to our children. They are our children; but even more, they are people. Each is a unique individual with needs, wants, desires, strengths and limitations; and, of course, the age of a child is a very important factor as has been mentioned in various contexts throughout this book.

The question, then, of family dynamics depends on who makes up the family. As adults, where are we along our own path of individuation, of self-knowledge and development? As a relating couple, where are we in trusting, loving and interacting? With our children, are we able to perceive their needs which are evolving as they grow. Are we able to be in touch with our inner child, who is often hurt, wounded and needy. When we can nurture our own inner child we can come into a better relationship with our mate and children.

Making Decisions

Making decisions is often not very easy for one single person and when it involves more than one person, the difficulty is often compounded. I have heard from a number of mature single people that one of their major reasons for not marrying is that they want to be their own boss; they don't want to give up their independence; they want to be answerable only to themselves and they treasure their independence.

All that may be so, but what is missing is the challenge and the rewards of forging decisions in the heat and glow of the hearth of interpersonal relationships. Surprisingly, many decisions are easier made when there is more than one point of view. To put out my view of the matter and then find that there is an equally valid,

valid, even though quite different view that can be just as persuasive, can be exciting and stimulating. And further, that from those two views may come yet another solution which can be entirely new, can complicate matters, but can also lead eventually to the truly creative answer to a given life question. If decision making in a family setting can be looked at in this way, it has, at least a starting point for successful resolution.

Christ's saying, 'Where two or more are gathered together in my name...' may shed light on this whole topic of decision making in a family, or anywhere else for that matter.

It is the human interaction, and the process by which a decision is made that is often more important than the decision itself. (That is not to say that reaching clear and sharp decisions is unimportant; on the contrary, all too often the inability to reach decisions in a timely manner creates personal and family crises of major proportions.) It is in the process of 'working things out' that we come closest to the other person, for we are needing to use all our sensitivity and understanding of who the other is, i.e., temperaments, type, style, needs, moods etc.. We become 'practical psychologists' when we encounter another, especially in decision making. The more conscious of ourselves and others we are, the more effective we may be in this process.

The highest ideal we can hold in decision making is to reach a consensus. In Latin consensus means 'to feel with' and that is the real key to a decision. If we can all 'feel with' (be in agreement with) the decision then it is one that is likely to hold. We will not only go along with it, but even more so, we are likely to actively support a decision that we can 'feel with.'

The great social mistake, that we have individualized from national politics and our historic traditions, is that aspect of democracy which declares that 'majority rules.' In the practical sense it matters little whether it is a majority or a larger, more powerful figure - it is the 'big guy' who wins. In a sense it is 'might makes right.' Actually it is that might wins even though it may not be right. 'Majority rules' means winners and losers which may be necessary on a vast social plane. In a smaller, more intimate setting if there are winners/losers there is a gradual breakdown of relationships because the majority (stronger) side as well as the minority (weaker) side all too soon are locked into fixed positions which make meaningful communication difficult. There are hurts, scars, grievances over past decisions and apprehension, fear and resentment over future situations.

In our current language 'they' has become a terribly sad and irritating pronoun. 'They' are destroying the economy. 'They' made the rules and I am only following them. 'They' are responsible for... Many people feel helpless and alienated because in themselves they lack the power to make decisions which affect themselves directly and intimately. Decisions on wages, working conditions, policy at work are beyond most of us, and where there may be input and participation it is often in an adversary situation, e.g. unions versus management where one side wins while the other side loses.

Hardly anywhere in our lives, except in our family setting is there the opportunity to experience a

142

participatory form of decision making. All our training and experience 'in the world' sets us up for competition rather than cooperation; for a win/lose conclusion rather than for consensus where things are worked through until all can 'feel with' the decision.

This kind of decision making means that everyone who participates in the process needs to take responsibility. There is no longer 'they' who made the big mistake - but it is now 'we' who reached this decision and if it is wrong, 'we' take the responsibility. We should be able to anticipate better decisions when we work in this way, but there is no fool proof formula for capturing our share of wisdom. We will still need to learn by trial and error with our mistakes often being our most stringent teachers. The great advantage is that all parties feel a part of the process; responsible for the results of the decision, more supportive of it and hence sharing a greater chance of success. Even more, there is a feeling of belonging. We are a valued member of a group in which all take responsibility for their deeds.

All of what has been said applies first and foremost to the man and woman whose primary relationship has gone into creating the family situation. Most of us would say - 'of course we share in making the decisions.' Yet, when we begin to look more closely, we see, even in many loving and good relationships, decisions being made in many subtle and various ways. We often use power to get our way - although it is (or may be) disguised in any number of ways.

Power can be sheer force and strength but most of us use power in far more subtle ways. Threats such as: 'if you don't do it I will...' are often used at moments of strife whereas at easier times it may be more humorous and playful, while still retaining a sting. The effects will be felt on either a conscious or (more likely) on an unconscious level. There are variations on this theme; whether it be attacking a weak point; seduction in one form or another or any other method that is aimed at getting one's point of view accepted by the other. In the long run, it undermines trust and confidence in the relationship. It establishes a pecking order and some one wins while the other(s) lose.

So the real challenge is to enter a dialogue with the consciousness necessary to express your point of view while at the same time being open enough to 'truly hear' what others are saying. One of the most difficult things to do is to 'truly hear.' This means to listen with complete openness to the other; not forming judgments, formulating answers, thinking about how to strengthen your own argument. Here we are asked to really listen so openly and intensely that we become one with what we are hearing and even further, we become one with the process behind what we are hearing. The thought and feeling process and the content itself are only imperfectly represented by the words spoken and we reach a much higher state of involvement with the other when we can be part of the process behind the words. Not easy! But it is something towards which to strive as it is a way of breaking away from our own 'locked in' position which creates barriers and obstacles to the formation of a union that transcends the sum of its parts. 'When two or more are gathered in my name...' points the way toward the raising of consciousness beyond the individual bound by heredity and environment (and genes) to the potential of a spiritual reality of a Christ-like light within. Interestingly, it is not alone, but in communion with others where we have this opportunity. If we can 'truly hear' and 'truly see,' we have the possibility to go beyond our lower self and find the Divine in the other. This is the basis for truly human interaction.

In entering the other's process and point of view fully and uncritically, we can begin to experience the world from viewpoints other than our own. It can be frightening and disconcerting at first to experience ways of feeling and thinking that are not like our own. The further realization that solutions to problems may be quite right and yet be different than what 'I' might have come up with is inwardly challenging. In fact, with active listening and intensive dialogue, the chance is increased that a solution to a given problem may emerge that is not 'mine' or 'yours' - but 'ours.'

One of the worst family situations to experience occurs when the adults fight over a difficult-to-make decision and the child or children somehow have a say, or are in the middle of the argument/discussion. Particularly with young children, it is important that the parent(s) know what they want and remain unified so that the decisions can be acted upon with support and cooperation. The young child looks to us with trust and awe and needs to see and experience strength arising out of clarity. We need to do our work singly and with our partner in order to come to clarity so that we can have the strength to do what is needed in a timely fashion,

Younger children do not need to be involved in decision making as a major part of their existence. Instead it is far more important that the three, four, five and six year old sees that parents are able to do this in a good healthy way. The example is important and gives children a model upon which to later fashion their own powers of decision making.

For the young child to be involved in making decisions prematurely taxes the undeveloped intellectual and logical powers of thought. When we look at what goes into the making of a decision we see that it involves having a contextual relationship to the elements that surround the decision. We need to know or at least have some idea of the consequences of the decision to be taken. A young child lives much more in the moment, without all this logical and sequential thought. For us as parents to draw upon, encourage or expect the child to make important decisions too early, is to tear at the child's natural stage of development. It is like wanting to pluck and eat a ripe apple when all we have on the tree before us is the apple blossom. The effects often are nervous and demanding children who find it hard to actually be at peace with the world around them.

Well meaning parents are often so proud that they involve their young children in most basic decisions. They hope that if the children are to grow up and be independent in their own thought, then they should get an early start. Often, the reverse is true! To hold, protect and nurture the force, energy and capacity you want to see developed, is far more effective than exercising it too early. What we tend to get is a dissipation of that energy and a lack of appreciation for the value of the qualities we were wanting to develop. It is much more appropriate, in dealing with the younger child, to take the lead, from our intimate knowledge of our child and to make those early decisions because we know what the child needs or wants. If we are correct, then all concerned are happy and there is a smooth flow in our lives. If our decision is not correct, we will know it and be able to learn from the mistake for the next time. We need to guard against becoming somewhat sentimental when we say that we have no right to impose ourselves on our children or that as we are so imperfect ourselves why should we presume to know best what our child may need or want. In answer to that, we need to have the courage, having taken the responsibility to bring a child into the world, to nurture it to maturity. A child is still unfinished and needs that help and guidance until a later stage.

A thought about the rights of children needs insertion here. The greatest right of children is to be recognized as human beings and to be treated with the love, care and respect to which each human being is entitled. It is a matter of the highest respect to recognize the capacities of each person. With the child we need to honour and love the various stages of development through which we all journey. Once again, it becomes a question of courage and responsibility to act out of love and knowledge of our children in such a way that they may, as adults, have had the appropriate models, experiences and nourishment of body and soul to be who they are meant to be.

147

As the child grows, so too must there be an increase and expansion in its role as an active and vital part of the family. As parents we need to learn to listen in a new way to what comes from our children of five, six, seven and eight years of age. In our modern society, even children in this age range are influenced by media (directly or indirectly through friends and relatives.) We find that the gently emerging personality begins to acquire tastes and desires that are somewhat premature. As discussed earlier, we have to stand by our own values and tastes as well as remain open to our child's wishes and wants. It is so easy to get caught in the trap of either saying a flat 'no' to Suzie's request or to feel somewhat guilty and then say 'yes' to something you don't feel right about. How painful that choice becomes and how difficult to find another way.

There is no easy answer to this often painful dilemma in which we may find ourselves. It takes a conscious, centered parent to handle a particular situation with finesse, with openness and most of all with a sense of humour. This is a tall order at any time. It also takes a lot of background work and preparation so that the relationship of parent and child is close enough, rich enough and filled with enough trust and respect so that neither parent nor child feels threatened in the moment. In other words, decision making ultimately depends on all the other elements of the relationship, i.e., love, trust, respect and devotion.

One way to build this relationship in addition to mutual decision making, is a regular time of sharing and communicating about things that are important to us. While the evening meal may be a time of telling what we each did at home, school and work, there

148

needs to be another time that is 'special;' this is a time for the 'family meeting.' It should be regularly scheduled and have its own particular mood which, of course, will vary from time to time. This is the time to share what will happen in the week to come i.e. Mummy will be out on Wednesday evening, Daddy will be out on Tuesday and Mummy and Daddy are going out to dinner on Saturday evening. John is going to a birthday party on Saturday afternoon and Monday, after school, there is a dentist appointment, and so on. This gives everyone a sense of what is happening and begins to give a model to the children of organizing their time so that they aren't disappointed in the last moment when they want to do something and find that it doesn't work out. It is an excellent time to allow the children (from about seven and older) to have a sense that they can have a say in some family affairs. 'I would like a friend to sleep over on Friday evening and could we get Janet to be the baby sitter on Saturday when you go for dinner?' This kind of gentle looking at the week-to-come involves everyone's participation and may well avoid some of the frantic moments that can all too easily come about in a busy family. It gives to all members of the family, old and young, a feeling that each has some part to play in the planning of the activities. Thus it isn't 'they' who did it, but 'we' may do it. [A word of caution; with younger children, before the eighth or ninth year, we have to be careful and not be too rigid. Don't expect much of a 'time sense' and sequential consistency. Use this as a gentle exercise that will lead toward these capacities.]

Another aspect of this regular family meeting, especially as the children pass their ninth year, is to take some time to reflect upon the past week and to

discuss what went well and where the rough spots may
have occurred. Here a special mood should be gradually
developed where each family member may feel free to
speak without the fear of reprimand. This should be a
time of discussion and reflection and not a time to be
pulled into an argument. Each family member; Mother,
Father and children need to develop listening skills -
to really hear what is trying to be expressed; the kind
of listening that can hear thoughts and feelings as well
as the actual words. It may be particularly hard for one
or another of the parents to relinquish the role of
authority for this short period of time. Actually, by so
doing and by being able to listen, speak and interact in
a free way, one's 'natural' authority rather than 'role
model' authority may be increased ten-fold.

Some examples:

1) Mother, to 11 year old Jane: 'I am sorry I
yelled at you yesterday after school - I had a
frantic day and I think I took some of that out
on you.'

2) John, (ten year old): 'Dad, I really wanted
that T-shirt with the picture of the guns on
it. Why couldn't I get that one instead of the
red one we finally bought?'
Dad: 'John, you know how I feel about the
clothes we wear. I feel they represent who we
are and what we have to say about ourselves. I
also resent clothes that have pictures of
commercial products on them as I don't feel
that I need to be a walking advertisement for
some product that isn't particularly good to
begin with. I really feel strongly about this
and I am sorry I spoke sharply to you in the

store. I also understand that you want to have what some of your friends have, so perhaps we need to think some more about this question. Do you have any suggestions John?'

4) Father, to 12 year old Carol: 'Carol, I want to thank you, once again, for all the help this week. You really stepped in and did some wonderful things when Mother and I were so busy. I really appreciate it'

These kinds of examples, with a more positive and constructive approach, allow for precious moments of true recognition and respect for each other. There may be times when less positive things are said, but much can be accomplished when we are conscious of remaining constructive as an inner and outer attitude.

The family meeting (or family circle) gives the chance for each to express himself; when it is started early enough, it allows for the formation and development of a channel of communication and understanding that is so vitally important as children enter adolescence. In counselling families with teenagers, I have seen many examples where the family meeting has been successful; but unless there is the possibility of good clear communication, no forum will solve the problems. It is the forum of the family meeting that allows the possibility for something to happen. Unless each person comes to the meeting with some openness and a willingness to share, then nothing, or possibly even less than nothing will take place.

Our role as decision makers in relation to our children is a gradually evolving one. As I have suggested earlier we are, at first, models of clarity, strength and honesty, imitated by the children in their first years. Then, until the advent of adolescence we need to gently and gradually guide our children to develop the skills of decision making by being consistent to our values, clear in our direction and loving in our understanding of how the child is affected by what we say and do, and how we, in fact, do and live in relation to our own standards. Because the child's developmental path is one which leads it gradually away from an unquestioning and completely trusting relationship with the parent, to one that is questioning and challenging, we as parents, also need to evolve. Our children's gradual withdrawal from us and their striving for independence is a natural and healthy process; although it is also one that is fraught with pain and difficulty. Children's challenge to you, as a parent, is hardly a personal affront. It is something through which we all go and have gone. It is a life long struggle toward individuation and is, in fact, the mission of this age in which we live. Rudolf Steiner calls it the 'consciousness soul age' and characterized it as a time when all people need to experience their own 'I' or individuality as fully and independently as possible. This is a lonely, challenging and painful struggle which serves as a preparation for the fulfillment of our mission on the earth which is to develop the force of love and brotherhood out of our true independence and our free individuality. These are high ideals and perhaps they suggest some reason that life becomes ever more challenging and complex. Parenting, therefore, affords us yet another way in our own life to become more conscious of that process of individuation. To go through the stage of being the role

152

model of authority for the young child to the gradual sharing of authority and decision making as our children mature, actually mirrors the history of humankind on this earth. From Priest/King in ancient days to democracy in the present, is something of the picture image that we can hold of the process of changing relationships between parent and child.

Adolescence

As our children approach adolescence, we are faced with a new reality and a new set of circumstances. Suddenly, we must share our space with people who are not only larger physically, but whose personalities and presence fill the space in a much more intrusive way. This happens at a time in our own lives (mid-to-late thirties) when we ourselves are needing more space (inner space.) For many parents, having to face the challenge of adolescent children comes just at the time in their own lives when they are being faced with inner crises of their own. Often the questions being asked by the teenager: 'Who am I? What do I want to be and do? Why is the world so full of inconsistency?' are just the questions we, as adults, are asking in perhaps a more profound way. At just the time when we are questioning our values, so too are our teenagers questioning the values society and their parents have imposed on them.

Perhaps one of the most difficult challenges of parenting is not to become defensive when we hear these questions. We need to experience the challenge to our old authority while we witness the teenager's sometimes chaotic search and experimentation. The all too easy patterns into which we may fall are either to reassert the old fashioned, stern authority which often creates a situation of resentment and alienation or to pull back in despair, believing that there is nothing to be done in relation to this volcanic energy and activity that is coming to meet us from our teenage children.

Childhood is a gradual process of incarnation; from the spiritual and physical germ; to the building of a body and growing into it as a personality; to the forming of a relationship to the world around it. Teenagers represent that point of having arrived at the present. They live fully in this world of today.
There is something like a magical
awakening to self
and the world around.
We as parents need
to make that extra effort
to meet our teenagers in 'the today.'
That is a delicate and subtle meeting
for we must be, once again, true to ourselves,
our standards, values, beliefs and experiences
and be willing more than ever before, to share
who and what we are. At the same time we need to be sincerely open and interested in what our teenage children have to bring to us. Often it will be inconsistent (just as we are accused of inconsistency,) garish, and in poor taste. Sometimes our teenagers will try to shock and test us in innumerable ways. Down deep, adolescents want to see who we really are; want to know our true being. Adolescence is a time of seeking out models, heroes; people to emulate. Although most teenagers, including ourselves, usually seek our models from farther afield than our parents - there is often that secret wish and hope that our parents are worthy of emulation.

In spite of all the outer actions, teenagers want and need consistency, limits, values and standards, and while often fighting them, they crave that which is so difficult for them to attain. As parents, we need to be there with a love that asks little or nothing in return. We need to keep a sense of humor even in the face of our own hurt and pain. We need to battle through some unpleasant scenes and yet be there in our love and support with an ever renewed freshness and enthusiasm. What is asked of us as parents, is sometimes more than we would expect of any person. That is as it should be; for as parents we have been given the wonderful challenge of growing as human beings while at the same time giving the highest service that is possible - to help in the creative process of bringing another human being into the world.

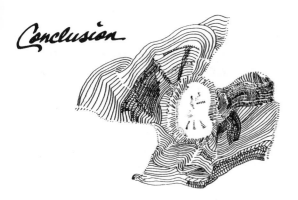

Conclusion

In the course of this short book, I have perhaps not given the exact answers and confident formulas that so many parents seem to be craving today. My strong feeling is that there are all too many easy answers nowadays and often they are not right for us in our particular circumstances. What 'works' for one person or in one set of circumstances is not necessarily what can be replicated over and over again. Underlying the giving of formulas for solving the problems of life, whether they be in parenting or in personal growth areas, is the assumption that human relationships can be improved through a 'scientific' approach.

Rudolf Steiner, on speaking about Waldorf education once said: "Waldorf Education is not a method. Rather it is an art of awakening. In order that the student be awakened the teachers must be on their own path of awakening themselves."

I believe that could well be our motto as parents. There isn't one method or technique for becoming a 'good' parent or to create a 'good' family. We need to approach the creation of a healthy family as an artistic life challenge. We have to deeply seek within ourselves for our own creativity, so that each and every situation will be met, by us, in much the same way as any artist would meet a blank canvas or a hunk of clay. What can we bring forth from this new situation that will be fresh, alive and creative?

If we are able to bring a background of thought, reflection, a healthy mood and a creative force, then we may well be able to solve the riddle that is presented to us - which is each and every time, unique. Having the right principles and a good technique allows for creative answers. If we have only a formula we are severely limited in its application. Living life is not a science, it
is an
art.

As artists, we need
nourishment of the soul
to keep us alive and creative.
We need to be seeking deep within
ourselves to find our creative wellsprings.
We need stimulation, encouragement, inspirations.
We need to be continually activated and reactivated
in such a way that our creative potential is stimulated
to rise to new heights of fulfillment.

As parents, we need to remember that we are people first and that in the long run we will be better parents as we become more creative and alive as people. The busier and more challenged we are in our role as parents, should be a signal that our own individual needs also must be met. Without the inner nourishment and refreshment, we cannot possibly do justice to our role as parent or spouse.

The purpose of this book has been to offer some thoughts and ideas about this whole complex area of creating a family as an artistic expression. I hope there have been some thoughts that may inspire. The highest work of creation is the human being – may we become creative participants in this endeavor!

Footnotes

1. Rudolf Steiner's Basic Books
   Theosophy, An Introduction to the Super-Sensible
   Knowledge of the World and the Destination of
   Man
   An Outline of Occult Science
   Christianity as Mystical Fact
   Knowledge of Higher Worlds and its Attainment
   Philosophy of Freedom

2. Kenneth Keniston & the Carnegie Council on Children;
   All Our Children: the American Family Under Pressure,
   New York, Harcourt Brace Jovanovich, 1977. See
   Chapter 1 for excellent discussion, The
   Transformation of the Family.

3. See the Essay, Thought on the Future of the Family,
   by Barrington Moore, Jr., in John N. Edwards, Editor,
   The Family and Change, New York, Alfred A. Knopf,
   1969.

4. From "Rock Me To Sleep" by Elizabeth Allen, quoted
   from Mary Cable, The Little Darlings: A History of
   Child Rearing in America, New York, Scribner, 1975,
   p. 95.

5. In various states of consciousness, time does indeed
   play interesting "tricks." While daydreaming, as
   well as in regular dreaming and sleep, we can lose
   all track of time. Think of how quickly a "good time"
   passes compared to the endless crawl of time in a
   boring or awkward situation. And in spatial terms
   just picture the huge rug to be vacuumed but the same
   tiny spaces for having all your friends over for a
   party.

6. James H. Bossard and Eleanor S. Boll, Ritual in
   Family Living, Philadelphia, University of
   Pennsylvania Press, 1950.

7. Bennett Olshaker, The Child As A Work Of Art, New
   York: Readers Digest Press, Dutton, 1975.

8. Ibid., pp. 99-100

9. Rudolf Steiner, Knowledge of Higher Worlds,
   Anthroposophical Press, Spring Valley, New York.

10. Rudolf Steiner, Prayers for Mothers and Children,
    Rudolf Steiner Press, London, 1968.

11. Ibid.

12. Kenneth Wydro, Flying Solo, Berkeley Publishing
    Corporation, distributed by G. P. Putnam's Sons, New
    York, 1978.

13. Ibid., 10